A GIFT FOR

....

FROM

....

THE SWEET TALK OF
Success!

HOW **35** AMAZING
WOMEN OVERCAME MAJOR
CHALLENGES IN LIFE

COUNTRYMAN

TODAY'S CHRISTIAN
woman

Published by J. Countryman, a division of Thomas Nelson, Inc, Nashville, Tennessee 37214.

Project manager—Terri Gibbs

All Scripture quotations are taken from the Holy Bible, New International Version. Copyright ©1973 International Bible Society. Used by permission of Zondervan Bible Publisher.

Designed by The DesignWorks Group, Sisters, Oregon.

ISBN 13: 978-1-4041-0408-9

www.thomasnelson.com
www.jcountryman.com
www.christianitytoday.com

Printed and bound in China

Contents

THE SWEET TALK OF
Success!

"As a young woman I was a very unhealthy person who made lots of destructive choices."

TODAY'S CHRISTIAN

woman

REAL STORIES • REAL ISSUES • REAL FAITH

SEPTEMBER/OCTOBER 2006

Bible study teacher
BETH MOORE
Catch her PASSION
for God's Word. PAGE 30

9 Ways to
Help Your Child
THRIVE in
Public School

TOUGH LOVE
Learning to forgive someone
who doesn't say "I'm sorry"

6 WAYS
to find more
time for prayer

DISCOVER
God's Gift of Rest
(It's waiting for you NOW)

FLEX APPEAL!
LIFTING WEIGHTS IS
GOOD FOR YOUR
BODY *AND* SOUL

NEVER SAY NEVER...
A coma survivor's
take on FAITH and
END-OF-LIFE DECISIONS

Beth Moore: Out of the Ashes of Childhood Abuse

nternationally known Bible-study teacher Beth Moore may don her husband Keith's hunting camouflage or unroll a laundry list of family dysfunctions to make a point. But fun isn't her main agenda; it's communicating the transforming power of Jesus and His Word to women.

Beth, I've seen you teach in person and on DVD. And in both you come across as very intense. Where did this intensity come from?

Even though I committed my life to Christ as a child, as a young woman I was a very unhealthy person who made lots of destructive choices. I didn't yet understand about God's Spirit living through me.

Having been raised in the church, I had memorized a fair amount of Scripture. But as far as God's Word empowering me to have the renewed mind of Christ and to live differently, I was a long way from that.

By the time I was married and in my mid-twenties, I had taught children's Sunday school classes, led a Christian fitness class, and done some speaking. When a position for an adult Sunday school teacher opened up, I went for it. But I was absolutely terrible at it.

I'd say something funny, then tack a Scripture onto it. How in the world did my first class ever put up with me? We had some fun together, but I'm not sure we learned anything.

When I read in my church bulletin about a Bible doctrine class on Sunday nights, I knew that, while the class would bore me to tears, God wanted me to go. At the first class, the teacher opened his Bible and taught us with such a passion that tears filled his eyes. When it was over, I ran to my car and burst into tears. "I don't know what that was," I told God, "but I want it."

That night God lit a fire in my heart for His Word that continues to this day. It wasn't until I fell in love with Jesus through His Word that the chains of sin began dropping off me.

What do you mean by chains of sin?

Being victimized as a child. I was very young when it started. My victimization wasn't constant, because my victimizer didn't have continual access to me. But it certainly was enough to mess me up at a time when I was figuring out who I was. I was pigeon-toed. I had buckteeth. I had the hairiest legs in the free world. Even though I did well in school, I had the worst self-esteem imaginable.

Many wonderful things happened to me as a child. I was loved. I was raised in the church. But I'm not convinced there's enough good to offset the devastation of abuse.

So what led you to Jesus?

After my freshman year in college, I was a camp counselor for sixth-grade girls. Early one morning, as the girls were sleeping, I sensed God's presence. There were no audible words, no bright lights. But suddenly I knew, without a doubt, that my future was entirely His. "You are now mine," He told me.

It took me a long time to break free from self-destruction. Yet even in those turbulent years, Jesus drew me back. I couldn't stand anything that put distance between Christ and me. I still can't. His presence is everything to me.

Have you confronted your past?

Yes, I went through a season of uncharacteristic despair in my early thirties. I'd never before looked straight at my victimization, never allowed my mind to replay the images. Every single time they began to erupt, I pressed them down.

But I no longer had the energy to do that. The victim in me took over. I felt like I was jumping off the highest cliff and descending into the bottom of a canyon. While my daughters knew I was sad, they didn't have an idea how severe it was. I was good at hiding it; you don't have my kind of background and not develop a way to do that.

Did you go through counseling?

Yes, I'm a big believer in sound, godly counsel. You don't go through what I went through and not get counsel. I needed someone to talk me through it. It was the worst season of my life. But God, in His goodness, brought fruit out of my turmoil and despair. Such fiery trials burn the fake out of us. For me, the fake was over. I didn't have the desire for it anymore.

What do you tell others struggling with grief or despair?

Grieve your loss, wrestle it out, throw a spiritual fit. But through those tears, allow the Word to reside in you. Psalm 126:5–6 says: "Those who sow in tears will reap with songs of joy. He who goes out weeping, carrying seed to sow, will return with songs of joy, carrying sheaves with him." Even when we think we'll never get over something, if we stay faithful, God promises we'll reap a harvest of joy. He'll never forsake us. That's why we've got to know His Word—so when our feelings don't match what we know to be true, we can still put one foot in front of the other.

—By Jane Johnson Struck, editor of *Today's Christian Woman*.
From *Today's Christian Woman*, September/October 2005.

Moving Beyond Abuse

1. The bitterly painful experiences will continue to hurt you if you don't cry out your pain to the Lord, release all that pain and bitterness to Him, and ask Him to help you forgive.

2. If you can't forgive another person it doesn't mean you aren't saved, and it doesn't mean you won't go to heaven. But it does mean you can't have all that God has for you and you will not be free of emotional pain. The first step to forgiving is to receive God's forgiveness. When we realize how much we have been forgiven, it's easier to understand that we have no right to pass judgment on one another.

3. God forgives you quickly and completely upon your confession of wrongdoing. You are to forgive others quickly and completely, whether they admit failure or not.

4. Forgiveness is a choice that we make. We base our decision not on what we *feel* like doing but on what we *know is right*. God's Word says, "Forgive, and you will be forgiven" (Luke 6:37).

5. There are both spiritual and psychological reasons to forgive. The spiritual reason is that we desire to obey God, and He has told us to forgive others just as He has forgiven us (Eph. 4:32). The psychological reason to forgive others is to free ourselves from the pain and victimization that other people have inflicted on us. When we forgive, we make a choice to no longer allow other people's sin to dictate how we feel or what we do.

—Stormie Omartian, *Seven Prayers That Will Change Your Life Forever,*
(J Countryman 2006). Used by permission.

"I was more afraid to say no to the Lord than I was to teach the class, despite my painful shyness."

TODAY'S CHRISTIAN

woman

Struggling with "SKIN-IS-IN"?
How to take the
**Fashion High Road
in a Low-Rise World**

**5 KEYS to Staying
Married**~when you
feel like calling it quits

**DETERMINE Your
Spiritual Specialty**

4 WAYS to Find Treasured
(and Trustworthy!)
Workplace FRIENDS

a **VISION**
of her own PAGE 54

Bible teacher **ANNE GRAHAM LOTZ,**
daughter of famous evangelist Billy Graham,
has launched REVIVALS for women
across the world.
DISCOVER the
desperate prayer
that started it all.

Anne Graham Lotz:
Overcoming Painful Shyness

R enowned Bible teacher Anne Graham Lotz started holding revivals because of her own desperate need for spiritual renewal. Here's what lies behind her passion to know Christ and make Him known.

Seeing you now, it's hard to believe that when you first started teaching the Bible, you'd become nauseated from nerves.

It's true. When I began teaching a Bible Study Fellowship class in 1976, I was painfully self-conscious. I was terrified to get up in front of the class with all eyes staring at me.

If it was so difficult for you, why did you plow ahead?

After my son, Jonathan, was born in 1970, followed by my daughters Morrow and Rachel-Ruth, I was immersed in small talk, small toys, small clothes, and small, sticky fingerprints. I found it hard to set aside time for Bible reading and prayer, much less my treasured morning cup of coffee. So I didn't. I wasn't drifting spiritually intentionally; I was distracted. But because the importance of prayer and Bible study had been ingrained in me from childhood, I desperately desired them.

I wanted to take a Bible Study Fellowship course, but nobody volunteered to teach it. Even though I'd never so much as taught a Sunday school class before, I was so desperate to be in BSF that I agreed to lead it. I not only had to complete the lesson plan, which involves daily Bible reading and studying, but I also had to prepare a weekly message.

Three hundred women showed up for the first meeting. I knew God had opened this door for me. I was more afraid to say no to the Lord than I was to teach the class, despite my painful shyness. Within a year, the class had grown to five hundred.

Does God expect us to do something we don't think is our spiritual gift?

Sometimes God calls us in our point of need. That's because God is attracted to our weakness. Where we're weak, He's strong. Where we're inadequate, He's sufficient. When we say we can't, we discover *He* can. In 1 Corinthians 1:27, 28, God says He chooses the weak and uneducated, the ones the world despises, because when He uses them and people's lives are changed, He receives the glory.

Why did you create Just Give Me Jesus revivals?

Again, because it was what I needed. In the late '90s, a series of events in my life left me crying out desperately to God. My heart cried out, "Just give me Jesus," because I felt that if I had a fresh encounter with Him, my questions about what was going on in my life either could wait, or *He* would be the answer. I opened my Bible and prayed, "God, I need a supernatural touch from you."

How did Jesus answer?

Through my study of the people Jesus touched in the Gospel of John. That study became the basis of my book *Just Give Me Jesus*. Then God gave me a burden for other women like myself, women raised in a Christian home and raised in the church, who needed to revive their passion for Jesus.

What do you hope to accomplish at the revivals?

I'm not interested in making a name for myself, building a ministry, or telling people what I think they need to hear. I'm more selfish than that: I want to *know* God. And I'm after the hearts of people so they can fall in love with the Lord.

How do we do that?

At the revivals, I share the practical tools I use to read the Scriptures. I ask the women to read a selected passage of Scripture, then to list the obvious facts in each of the verses, using the words in the passage. Then I ask them to determine what spiritual lessons or principles can be gleaned from these facts. Finally, I ask the women to write out those lessons in the form of a personal question, such as: *What does it mean in my life? Is there a command, warning, promise, principle, or example for me here in God's Word?*

These simple steps train the believer to listen to God's voice while reading the Bible. It's a beautiful, disciplined form of meditation on God's Word. This is vital for spiritual health because the way you know God is by reading His Word.

But it's also vital to talk to Him on your knees in prayer. As you grow in your relationship with Him through communication, you need to further flesh out that knowledge through obedience. You can say "Jesus is Lord," but words mean nothing. The proof of His Lordship in your life is your obedience to His commands.

One of the first verses I memorized was Philippians 4:6: "Do not be anxious about anything, but in everything, by prayer and petition, with thanksgiving, present your requests to God." A friend cross-stitched that for me because I'm a worrier. Worry is in my genes.

Our spiritual success is directly related to being in the Book. That helps us keep our focus. *We* tend to look at things in light of how we feel today and what we think can happen tomorrow. But *God* sees the big picture; He knows that if we can just get our eyes off this moment and hold on, down the road there will be tremendous blessing.

—By Jane Johnson Struck, editor of *Today's Christian Woman*.
From *Today's Christian Woman*, May/June 2003.

Jumpstart Your Passion for God's Word

1. *Remember the Bible's benefits.* Just as satisfying physical craving releases feel-good chemicals in our brains, satisfying our hunger for Scripture releases all kinds of spiritual benefits and blessings in our lives, such as increased wisdom, comfort, and peace.

2. *Make daily Bible reading a habit.* Decide on a reading plan, and commit to spending time in God's Word *every* day, whether you feel like it or not. After following that plan for a few weeks, I found I couldn't skip a day in Bible reading without feeling deprived.

3. *Keep a spiritual journal.* Keep a record of what you read in the Bible and how it influences your life. Use a spiral notebook, or simply jot down notes in your Bible. You will soon see how Scripture has touched your heart, motivated change, or given you insight into life's circumstances.

4. *Customize study to fit your personality.* For years I struggled to read through the Bible in a year. Finally, I realized that plan just didn't fit me. Now I tailor study to my personality, allowing more in-depth studies and careful reading of shorter passages.

5. *Customize study to fit your circumstances.* A mother of preschoolers might not be able to devote the same amount of time and energy to reading God's Word as a mom with kids in school. Make sure you're not demanding too much for your circumstances.

—Katrina Baker, *Today's Christian Woman*, July/August 2004.

"I learned there's freedom in not having to be in control all the time."

TODAY'S CHRISTIAN

woman

MAY/JUNE 2004

WOMEN JUST WANT TO HAVE FUN!
And former *Facts of Life* star
LISA WHELCHEL
is helping them find time to do just that. PAGE 38

REAL STORIES • REAL ISSUES • REAL FAITH

Is ENVY Robbing
YOU of Girlfriends?

TOUGH
QUESTIONS
All Singles Ask

TOO BUSY
to Journal?
5 FRESH
APPROACHES
that won't overwhelm you!

INTIMACY
After Impotence:
HOW TO
KEEP YOUR
LOVE
ALIVE

U.S. $3.95 Canada $5.50

Lisa Whelchel: Giving Up the Need to Be in Control

Lisa Whelchel, the woman probably best known for her role as sassy rich girl Blair Warner in the '80s sitcom *The Facts of Life*, has since acquired a reputation as author of several books and creator of MomTime Get-A-Ways weekend conferences for stressed moms (in partnership with Lifeway). Lisa shares a few thoughts on how she's learned to get real in her life and to let go of her need to be in control.

How did MomTime Getaways begin?

Years two through seven were really tough in my marriage. I had lost all of my earnings from *The Facts of Life* as well as our house because of bad investments. Steve and I had three children in three years. Tucker, Haven, and Clancy were 3, 2, and 1 at the time. Taking them out in public in Los Angeles was miserable.

Yet staying in all day was miserable, too. I was desperate for some adult conversation. So I invited my mom and two church friends to join me for a weekly gathering to eat lunch and play games—I'm a closet board-game lover—while our kids napped or played together in another room. The women jumped at the idea, and the first MomTime group was born.

These gatherings became a life source for us. The laughter, food, and talk were natural stress relievers. By the time our gatherings were finished, we were ready to go tackle another week.

We invited other friends to join us, and eventually other MomTime groups formed.

What happened next?

The time seemed ripe for expanding the MomTime vision. My husband, Steve, an experienced conference planner for our church's denomination, helped me stage the first MomTime Get-A-Ways conference in Nashville, Tennessee, in 2002.

Two-hundred fifty women showed up, many of whom had gotten to know us through the daily Internet journal that I kept when my family and I toured the U.S. in an RV the year before. This first Friday-night and all-day Saturday event was a time of encouragement, parenting tips, prayer, reprieve from the usual mom duties, plenty of playtime, and lots of chocolate. The women seemed to need to be little girls again and to just play.

What deeper needs do you see women struggling with?

I think we wrestle with control issues. We think it's up to us that our kids turn out OK, our marriage thrives, and our future is successful. We need to be responsible for the people and things entrusted to us, but ultimately *God* is in control. There's such freedom in releasing that control into His hands. My goal is to show these women they need to trust God in all things.

The concept of giving up control isn't one that has come easily to me. I began calling the shots in my life at age twelve, when I landed my first television role as a Mouseketeer on the *New Mickey Mouse Club*. It was a job that required me to move away from home.

What effect did your take-charge personality have on your marriage?

The take-charge personality was good for my childhood acting career, but it wasn't so healthy for my marriage. I usually would make family decisions before Steve, my detail-oriented husband, even had a chance to chime in. Although the family ran smoothly, Steve and I were miserable

Things got so bad between Steve and me that divorce started to sound appealing. This is when I began to pray earnestly for direction and healing. First I sensed God nudging me to acknowledge all the good things Steve brought to our relationship and our family instead of focusing on what I thought he did wrong.

How did you let go of your need to be in control?

As I began to focus on Steve's strengths and to affirm them verbally, I started to see healing in our relationship. I hadn't realized how much my negative words had wounded him. But when I started to praise Steve, even when I didn't necessarily feel like it, he had a new joy and confidence. That made affirmation easier to give—and paved the way for my next adventure: a decision-making fast.

I sensed God leading me to stop making decisions for forty days. I wanted Steve to be the leader in our home, but God helped me see that I needed to get out of Steve's way so he could lead. So instead of jumping in and making financial, parenting, or time-management decisions for the family, I stepped back for forty days and said to Steve, "Whatever you think is best, honey."

Wasn't that terribly difficult for both of you?

Of course! Steve wasn't used to calling the shots for our family. There were times when he made decisions I wouldn't have, when I knew the outcome wouldn't be the best. One decision led us to lose money, but even then I learned a valuable lesson. I was reminded how everything we have comes from God.

When Steve made what looked like a poor decision, God brought the situation to a positive end. Once Steve realized that even when he made bad decisions I wasn't going to leave or say "I told you so," that brought healing to our marriage. Submitting to him and letting him use his gifts has been such a blessing to our family. I learned there's freedom in not having to be in control all the time. And I learned that ultimately I'm not just trusting in my husband, I'm trusting in God.

—By Camerin Courtney, managing editor of *Today's Christian Woman*.
From *Today's Christian Woman*, May/June 2004.

How a Wife Can Say, "I Love You"

- *Show respect.* Respect is not optional; it's *essential* in a healthy marriage. Thank God for what is right about your man, not what is wrong. God will hold your husband accountable for the condition of the home, so respect that position of responsibility.
- *Offer trust.* As a wife follows the leadership of her husband, that expression of trust becomes a powerful act of love. It says, "I believe in you." It's only possible to trust your husband if your ultimate trust is in the Lord, who calls you to follow the lead of the man he has brought into your life.
- *Provide support.* A man feels loved when his wife says, "Wherever you go and whatever you do, I'm in. You can count on me." But there is a fine line between supporting and mothering. Men love support but often pull away from unsolicited assistance, which makes them feel less than adequate.
- *Offer acceptance.* The key is to *communicate*, not *nag*. Share your ideas, concerns, fears, or expectations, then leave it alone. Give God a chance to work and your husband time to change. When you offer acceptance, approval, and affirmation, feedback will fall on receptive ears.
- *Love him.* For men, affection begins with respectful admiration and builds with sincere appreciation, but the sexual relationship best says, "I love you." Of course, the beauty of this mysterious act of love is that the more you give, the more you're likely to receive.

—H. Dale Burke, adapted *from Different by Design* (Moody Press, 2000). Used by permission.

"My view of sex had been tainted by my premarital activity."

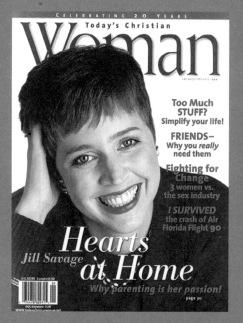

CELEBRATING 20 YEARS

Today's Christian

Woman

January/February 1998

Too Much STUFF?
Simplify your life!

FRIENDS—
Why you *really* need them

Fighting for Change
3 women vs. the sex industry

I SURVIVED
the crash of Air Florida Flight 90

Hearts at Home
Jill Savage
Why parenting is her passion!
page 30

U.S. $3.95   Canada $5.50

AOL Keyword: TCW
www.todayschristianwoman.net

Jill Savage: When a Husband Struggles with Pornography

Jill Savage, founder and director of Hearts at Home, an organization that encourages and educates women in the profession of motherhood, is passionate about helping moms. But she also wants to help women develop strong, Christ-centered marriages, which are the foundation of successful parenting. Jill, a mother of five, talks about how tough times in her marriage have helped her and the women she ministers to.

What type of family did you grow up in?

Any time the church doors were open, our family was there. But in high school I rebelled by partying, drinking, and dating non-Christians, all while still going to youth group.

Were you and Mark sexually active before you married?

Yes, I'm sad to say we were. And our sexual pasts definitely played a role in some of the problems we've faced in our marriage. For instance, most of what Mark knew about sex he learned from pornography. His exposure to pornography started at an early age and continued until we were married. The images became so ingrained in him that Mark didn't know there was any other way to relate sexually.

What prompted the turnaround?

While Mark was going to a Bible college, a fellow student sat him down and said, "I've struggled with some of the same things you're struggling with. I'd like you to know the healing I found. Would you consider going to a counselor?"

Mark went for counseling for two years. Then, we started counseling together. What we learned was eye-opening. For example, even though Mark's pornography use stopped as soon as we got married, we hadn't realized how it affected him. Mark's sexual demands of me were so unrealistic that I could never meet them. So I withdrew.

Mark had to rid his mind of pornography. How did you have to change?

I realized I was seeking refuge from a marriage I didn't like by focusing on my role as mom. I had to learn to be a wife to Mark first and a mother second.

I also discovered my view of sex had been tainted by my premarital activity. And, like my husband, I didn't have good conflict resolution skills because I had never seen them in action. So Mark and I began learning them together in counseling. I also became friends with another mom of small children; she became my confidante.

Wasn't it scary to open up?

Yes! I'd been keeping our situation a secret so long. Outwardly, we looked like a young Christian couple who had it all together, while inside our four walls were falling apart. I finally reached the point where I was dying inside; I had to talk it out with someone.

About a year later, I shared my situation with the other women who attended our moms group. There were lots of tears, but I said, "This is what we're working through. God is being faithful. But it has been really hard." That's when our moms group started to take off. People respond to honesty.

What's your relationship with Mark like now?

Mark is my best friend, and I love that. Do we still have struggles? Yeah, but now we have the tools to work through them. What I discovered was that when I stopped pointing the finger at Mark and started pointing it at me, our relationship improved. Instead of praying, "God, change him," I began praying, "God, change me." As God began to change me, I backed off Mark's case. He didn't have to spend as much time defending himself and was able to work on the changes God was asking him to make.

In what ways are the walls of your marriage still under construction?

When we bought our farmhouse, it was run-down and dirty, but we envisioned it as something beautiful. It was the same way with our marriage. When things were ugly, we could still envision it being better. And we operated from that vision. But we're still in the refining process.

That's why I'd love to be able to sit down with every woman who comes to a Hearts at Home conference and tell her that her emotions and her struggles are normal, that she's not alone, and that ultimately, through God's power and the encouragement of others, she too can experience fulfillment in marriage.

What kind of impact have you made through Hearts at Home?

We had more than 250 women come to the Lord once at a Bloomington conference. Because we focus on motherhood, our audience isn't necessarily all Christian; there are lots of women seeking encouragement and information on parenting. While we don't offer a formal invitation to accept Christ, we always try to communicate the message that through Jesus' death and resurrection, you can become part of God's family. We introduce women to their need for Christ and tell them that it's in Him they'll find their true self-worth.

—By Jane Johnson Struck, editor of *Today's Christian Woman*.
From *Today's Christian Woman*, January/February 1999.

Avoiding Online Pornography

The Internet has made pornography and fantasy relationships more convenient and more anonymous than ever before. By using common sense and a few technological safeguards, such as the following, you can avoid the snare of Internet infidelity.

1. Set up your computer in an open area of your home.
2. Don't cruise the Internet when you are tired, lonely, or feeling misunderstood.
3. Have a specific destination in mind when you go online.
4. Turn off the Instant Message system (if you use America Online), and turn on parental control tools and filtering software to block so-called adult sites, news groups, and chat rooms.
5. Remove your personal profile from online services to minimize your chances of attracting pornographic e-mail.
6. Recognize that conversing online with strangers steals time and energy from your marriage. Limit Internet usage to predetermined tasks, and spend more time conversing with your spouse.
7. Talk to a trusted friend about your temptations and failures. Ask that person to hold you accountable.
8. If you are overly susceptible to Internet trysts or online pornography, cancel your Internet access.

—Adapted from an article by John W. Kennedy in *Computing Today* magazine, January/February 1998. Used by permission.

"One reason we're so hard on ourselves is that we worship at the altar of other women's approval."

TODAY'S CHRISTIAN
YOUR LIFE · YOUR FAITH · YOUR WORLD
WOman

Bible study author
LISA HARPER
gets real about life, love, and
what we're truly longing for

7 Myths About
Forgiveness
(Which one is holding you back?)

WHEN *CHILDREN*
HAVE CHILDREN
What one ministry's
doing to help

Yada
Yada
Yada . . .
Why a best-selling novel
is inspiring women
to pray together

LOVE THE SKIN
YOU'RE IN!

HOW TO PLAY
FOR KEEPS IN
YOUR MARRIAGE

Lisa Harper: Breaking Free from the Need for Approval

There's just something about my black leather jacket and Harley-Davidson motorcycle that makes minivan-driving moms frown in disapproval," says Lisa Harper with a laugh. "The funny thing is, I'm usually riding to a Bible study!" Lisa, former women's ministries director for Focus on the Family, where she developed Renewing the Heart women's conferences, has since put her storytelling gifts, Bible knowledge, and humor to work creating *On the Road with Lisa Harper* (Tyndale), a series of Bible-study books with interactive DVDs. Here's what this author, speaker, and Bible teacher says about following God beyond other people's expectations.

You've raised some eyebrows by riding a motorcycle.

A lot of women tease me that they're nice to bikers now because they're afraid one might be me! [Laughs.] There's this stereotype of what a Christian woman should look like—and it doesn't include leather and Harleys. It has more to do with baking casseroles or being peppy or—

Being a size 2?

Right! We women are so hard on ourselves. We get so preoccupied with our culture's standards that we don't take the time to consider that

God isn't more pleased with us if we're a size 2. He sees us through the rose-colored glasses of Jesus and thinks we're absolutely beautiful.

I love the word *marinating*. We need to marinate in the truth of who God is and how He feels about us. That's why I wrote the study on the Old Testament book Song of Solomon.

Was it awkward writing on overtly sensual passages?

A friend's husband asked me why I would write on Song of Solomon, implying, "What's a single girl like you doing writing on this erotic poetry?" I said it was kind of like a dieter standing outside Krispy Kreme watching donuts go through the glaze machine!

Seriously, we tend to forget the gospel is about a supernatural, mind-blowing relationship with the Lord. In Song of Solomon 4:9, God says through Solomon, "You have stolen my heart with one glance of your eyes." Think about that: The God of the universe is enamored with us. That's huge. We wouldn't say this in Bible study, but somewhere in our crooked human hearts we assume God loves us because it's His job. He's compelled because He's the Creator and we're the created.

But God delights in us. His behavior toward us isn't reserved, rigid, formal. He condescends to make Himself available to us. He runs toward us. He longs for us to come to Him with affection and abandon. And He wants us to find our satisfaction in Him.

How do we find that satisfaction?

I recently read a book called *Addictions: A Banquet in the Grave* by Edward Welch. It deals with every addiction imaginable. I'll never forget one thing the author wrote: "Ultimately all excessive behavior is a disorder of worship." One reason we're so hard on ourselves is that we worship at the altar of other women's approval. We want to appear pretty and smart, to have perfect hair, and to have all the answers at Bible study so others will pat us on the back. Well, we aren't supposed to seek their approval. We're supposed to dance before the altar of God's approval.

What have you personally learned about finding approval?

That busyness isn't a spiritual gift. I really wrestle with that. God's teaching me my default setting shouldn't be stuck on "go."

I love Zephaniah 3:17, "He will rejoice over you with singing." Sadly, I've missed many of the lyrics God sings over me because I assumed that being busy juggling so many things pleases Him. Years went by where I didn't hear God's delight because I was listening to different music in my head.

What do you mean?

I grew up in a great church, but it definitely emphasized conforming to religious standards. I was a believer, but I knew God more as Abba Father than as Lover of my soul.

My father left when I was young, and my mother remarried. After my brother developed a substance-abuse problem, I watched my mom change from a fill-in-the-blanks kind of Christian to one whose relationship with God had rawness and authenticity. That made me long for more authenticity in my walk with the Lord.

Would you like to be married someday?

Of course! But I don't have too many dreamy ideals about the knight in shining armor, especially after being set up with everybody from grandpas to gropers.

I do want to be a mom. There are times when I'm a big whiny baby and complain, "God, didn't you see me the day you gave out the gift of marriage and children?" But most days, I love my life. I'm not eager to be married; I am eager to be in the middle of God's will, whatever that looks like.

The peace I have is the peace God gives me. I encourage women to run to the Lord with their lack of contentment. God meets us where we're broken. When our heart feels like it's been run over by a Mack truck, He brings comfort.

What do you want to accomplish most?

I long for women—from Nashville to Nairobi—to focus more on their relationship with God than with being appropriately religious.

Theologian Francis Schaeffer once said, "Our calling is to be not only a faithful bride but also a bride in love." That's what I want—to be the bride in love. I don't want to just memorize a bunch of facts about the Lord. I want to be so absolutely in love with Jesus that it permeates every facet of my being. I want to reflect the gospel as best I can in this crooked jar of clay.

—By Jane Johnson Struck, editor of *Today's Christian Woman*.
From *Today's Christian Woman*, July/August 2006.

Making the Most of Singleness

- *Ask Around.* Talk to your married friends and find out what they miss most about being single. Is it girls' nights out? Is it no longer having time to take a photography class? Take advantage of these opportunities now so you'll have no regrets later.
- *Make a List.* What do you want to accomplish in life—write a book? Travel to Italy? Go on a short-term missions trip? Write down your goals on a master list, then pick one thing and go for it. Don't let your life go on hold while you're waiting for a husband.
- *Pray.* Ecclesiastes 3 tells us there are specific purposes for certain seasons of life. Ask God what unique things He wants you to do or learn in this season of being single. Obedience to these things will draw you closer to God and give you an exciting ride.
- *Invest in Others.* Since you're not focusing your relational energy on a husband, you've got a lot to give others. There are Sunday school classes, refugee families, and weary neighbors who could be eternally blessed by your involvement in their lives. And the joy you receive in return will help chase away those lonely days.
- *Get Going.* There's a lot to see and do in this big world and now's your best chance to take it all in. A road trip with friends is always a bonding experience. And it's never too late for a family vacation. Enrich your life by expanding its boundaries. You never know who you'll meet along the way!

—Camerin Courtney, *Today's Christian Woman*, September/October 1998.

"It's okay to notice people's color; just don't stop there. See color, appreciate it, and celebrate it."

TODAY'S CHRISTIAN

woman

What EASTER Means for *You!*

Overcoming Breast Cancer
One survivor's strategies

6 FUNNY MONEY-SAVERS

Get a Group!
Why it can change your life

singer/songwriter **NICOLE C. MULLEN** on

THE SURPRISING WAY
HER MUSIC'S
BUILDING BRIDGES

page 44

$2.95 Canada $3.50

AOL Keyword: TodaysChristianWoman
www.TodaysChristianWoman.net

Nicole C. Mullen:
A Song for Racial Harmony

After winning the 2001 Song of the Year Dove Award for her sweeping ballad of faith, "Redeemer," making her the first African American to win in that prestigious category, Nicole C. Mullen has sung at several churches across the United States that never before had invited a black performer.

But issues of racial unity are close as home to her. Her husband, David, is white; their biological daughter, Jasmine, is biracial; and their adopted son, Maxwell, is full-blooded African American, just like Mom. Here's what Nicole has to say about racial unity and the adoption of her son, Max.

How were you transformed from a "bony-kneed girl" to a Dove-Award winner?

If I tried to take credit for my success, I'd be lying. I'm acutely aware that any success I have is from God. Unless God says, "This is your time," you can strive all you want and nothing will happen. Over the years I've released independent albums, toured as a backup singer, written songs for other people. Right now I feel like I'm having a God season. But I'm still ordinary. God is just choosing to use me in a more public way at this time.

He's using me to build bridges between different cultures and colors. Many times when I've sung about racial issues in a place that has never before had an African-American performer, people tell me after the concert, "We haven't ever talked about racial issues in our family, but we want to address them now."

Sometime last year when I performed live on a radio station, the DJ took calls from listeners between songs. One caller admitted he'd once been a racist. He asked for forgiveness and told me he loves my music and has bought one of my albums.

People being receptive to my music and the things I say between songs is a "God thing." Also, I try hard to communicate a message of racial unity without malice. If I talked about these issues with a chip on my shoulder, no one would listen. But I want others to see that diversity is good.

What else do you communicate about racial issues?

I love talking about history, both the good and the bad. I think we're called to learn from history so we don't repeat its mistakes. During slavery, good white people and bad white people existed, as did good black people and bad black people. The color of your skin doesn't make you good or bad; it's the condition of your heart. When it comes down to it, everybody, no matter what their skin color, needs Jesus.

I love to say, "I'm the great, great, great, great-granddaughter of a slave. In order for my family to have endured, they had to be strong physically, spiritually, and mentally." So I come from good stock.

I'm proud of that. But I'm even prouder that because I'm a Christian, my spiritual lineage now goes back to Abraham, Isaac, and Jacob."

Sure. I've been the brunt of racial slurs now and then. I've heard that some radio stations won't play my songs because of the color of my skin. There's still a need to promote racial unity in Christian circles. But at the same time, some people and stations have defied expectations by embracing me and my music.

How can you forgive those who judge you by the color of your skin?

First, I realize most racial slurs or negative assumptions are based on ignorance. People are often fearful of unfamiliar things.

Next, I realize how much God has forgiven *me*. So many times I've deserved a swift kick in the rear, and instead God has embraced me, even blessed me, which breaks me even more. He has shown me so much grace and mercy that I'm compelled to pass it on to others.

What do you say to your children about the diverse colors in your family?

My kids have always been color conscious. Jasmine says Max and I are brown, she's tan, and Papa's pink (he just loves that!).

I've always told her that when God made us, He said, "Now what would be Nicole's best color?" And God decided I'd look best brown. He decided tan would be Jasmine's best color, black would be Max's best color, and white would be Papa's best color. God made us the colors we are on purpose.

So it's okay to notice people's color; just don't stop there. See color, appreciate it, enjoy it, and celebrate it. Our family looks different than most, but we love that.

We both work in the Christian music industry. We met at the Gospel Music Association's annual conference in Nashville and attended a concert together one night with some mutual friends. We had great conversations about faith, racial issues, financial matters— you name it. Over time, David and I became best buddies.

I had been told not to marry somebody you can live with, but rather someone you can't live without. And the latter was definitely true with David.

Did racial issues surface when you started dating? How?

At first I was the one with the biggest hang-ups. When David and I would go out, I'd say, "Oh, those people are looking at us. We can't hold hands in public." But David would say, "Get over it." It came down to me realizing we didn't need to ask for anyone's permission to be together.

How did your respective families respond to your racial differences?

Our relationship was a non-issue for our immediate families. It was wonderful. I knew that when David and I had kids, we'd have great love and support from both sides, and that has definitely been the case. Actually, it's amazing to realize that since David only has sisters, our little African-American adopted son, Max, is carrying on the Mullen name for this white family.

—By Camerin Courtney, managing editor of *Today's Christian Woman*. From *Today's Christian Woman*, March/April 2002.

Teaching Kids about Race

- *One way to teach kids about race is to expose them to different cultures.* Big cities are wonderful cultural centers. They offer parades, festivals, art museums, and other multicultural events. You can find events listed in your local newspaper or posted at the library, or you can contact your state's ethnic affairs department.
- *Suggest that your child invite someone of a different race over to play.* It's an opportunity for your child to make another friend and for you to become acquainted with the parents of the child.
- *Teach your children about their own ethnic heritage.* It's difficult to affirm in other people what's never been affirmed in you. Everybody is ethnic! Caucasians need to recognize their own diversities and learn about their family's heritage, whether it's German, Swedish, Greek, English, Irish, or whatever.
- *Encourage schools and churches to teach racial reconciliation.* Urban public school systems deal with diversity all the time. Some have provided sensitivity training for teachers because it's hard to ask teachers to lead something they aren't familiar with. We need racial reconciliation to be a part of our school systems and churches so it can be incorporated into curriculum in a natural way.

—Brenda Salter McNeil. From *Christian Parenting Today*, March/April 2002.

"I realized there was nothing I could do to fix my broken family, so I suffered in silence."

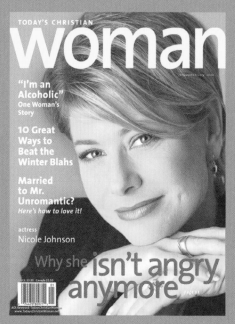

TODAY'S CHRISTIAN

woman

january/february 2004

"I'm an Alcoholic" One Woman's Story

10 Great Ways to Beat the Winter Blahs

Married to Mr. Unromantic? Here's how to love it!

actress Nicole Johnson

Why she isn't angry anymore

U.S. $3.95 Canada $5.50

AOL Keyword: TodaysChristianWoman
www.TodaysChristianWoman.net

Nicole Johnson: Freedom from Destructive Anger

A ctress Nicole Johnson looks very "together." But her frequent temper outbursts fractured her relationship with her mother and frayed her marriage. After a volatile argument with her former husband, Paul, Nicole finally realized how deep-seated anger was poisoning her relationships. With the help of a Christian counselor, she peeled back the layers of hurt that have plagued her since childhood.

Definitely. I think anger is hard for women to admit. There's a stigma attached to it. Men are considered powerful when they're angry, but women are called irrational or out of control.

But my anger shouldn't have come as a surprise. It had been staring me in the face for a long time; I just didn't want to own it. None of us do. But when you stand in front of the dryer completely reduced to tears because you can't find the mate to your black sock or you blow up in the grocery store because Starbucks ice cream is out of stock, you may need to admit you're not really angry about socks or ice cream.

Much of it stemmed from unresolved issues in my childhood. My parents divorced when I was six, ripping apart the family. My mother, brother, sister, and I moved from Florida to Louisiana. My father made the seven-hour drive to visit us as often as he could. We'd have joyful reunions and agonizing good-byes. There's no way to explain divorce to a child. It's pure, undiluted pain.

Then Mom and Dad began vying for our loyalty. As a child, I was placed on a witness stand and asked if I wanted to live with my mom or my dad. It was an impossible choice, but I said I wanted to live with my mother.

Unfortunately, it wasn't a final decision. I was forced to choose again and again. If I wanted to invite my dad to something significant, such as a birthday or my high-school graduation, my mother wouldn't attend. Often, Dad wouldn't make it anyway. As I got older, I realized there was nothing I could do to fix my broken family, so I suffered in silence. But one day after my blow-up with Paul, I broke the silence. I finally voiced my pain and anger.

I wrote Mom a letter. It had been a year and a half since we'd spoken. I went through four drafts, and the process took a couple of months. In my letter I told Mom about the road to healing I was on and invited her to come to Nashville to meet with my counselor and me. I wanted a relationship with her, I told her, but what we'd had in the past wouldn't work for me anymore. I told her that if she'd be willing to meet with us, we could try to forge a new path.

She wrote back, saying that of course she'd come and that she knew it would be a painful but needed process. And she told me she loved me. There was no trace of anger in her response. God must have softened her heart because she was more open than I'd ever known her to be.

We met with my counselor for three days. Mother had hurts I'd never known about. She talked about the emotional pain of her marriage breakups. We held each other. She saw the things she'd handled inappropriately and the ways she had tried to control my life over the years, and she asked for forgiveness. I realized how angry and withdrawn I had become and asked for Mother's forgiveness. She lavished it on me.

The highest compliment I can give is to say we're great friends. She has become a confidante and a counselor, a shopping buddy and a traveling companion. She's not the same woman I grew up with. Her faith has come alive after decades of dormancy. She's a loving grandmother and an active member of her church.

My mother and I are living proof that it's never too late to begin again. Our relationship isn't perfect; we still have our days, and we always will. But we're seeking to be honest with each other and keep short accounts. God's healing power is amazing. We're all looking for someone to fix us and help us and meet our greatest needs. But it doesn't happen apart from God.

Part of our hope in going through such a difficult process (I called it re-breaking the relationship bone to set it straight) was that Mom and I wouldn't have to go through it again, and that has proved correct. We've continued to build on the honesty and authenticity we sought to have with each other and it has made our relationship stronger than ever.

How about the relationship with your father—has that been restored?

My father and I have a wonderful relationship. He had a few health challenges recently that scared us all, but he's doing much better. It's amazing how the fear of losing someone you love brings a new perspective to the relationship—it's a dark gift, but I'm thankful for it. He's a great man.

How has releasing the fuel behind your anger freed you?

Part of what fueled my anger was a lack of control. When there are so many things outside of your control as a child or outside of your perceived control as an adult, internal anger is fueled. But to become responsible in your relationships is to realize that you have a lot of power, which is a good thing, properly understood. We have the power to communicate our feelings, to change things, and to make good choices. That goes a long way in diffusing anger.

Do you still blow up occasionally?

I still get angry at times, but it is very different now. I can choose anger as a response to something like injustice, and I do. But it's no longer an automatic response that I can't control.

—By Camerin Courtney, managing editor of *Today's Christian Woman*.
From *Today's Christian Woman*, January/February 2000.

Putting the Brakes on Anger

The next time you're about to fly off the handle, ask yourself these three questions. They can become an effective tool for maintaining self-control.

1. *Is my anger out of proportion to the circumstance?* While there may be a legitimate basis for anger, often our anger far outweighs the offense. Disproportionate anger makes resolution difficult, if not impossible. For anger to have healthy results, it needs to be reasonable and thus controllable.

2. *Is the momentary release I'll get from expressing my anger worth the long-term havoc it will wreak?* The very nature of anger promotes exaggerated emotions. We say and do things we never would otherwise. Those words and actions never can be undone. Whatever hasty words are spoken in the heat of an angry exchange never lose their power to wound.

3. *Is my anger worth dragging other uninvolved people into it?* Anger invariably affects the people around you. It's human nature to take sides even when you're not involved. But to allow outside parties to be drawn into your anger is a cheap way to feed your ego and justify poor behavior. Anger is usually a self-centered emotion. Your attention is turned inward on the wrong you've suffered, the wound you've sustained. By contrast, the principle of selflessness is woven consistently throughout the entire Bible: viewing others as more important than yourself (Philippians 2:3) and dying to your desires and your wounds (Matthew 16:24).

—Mayo Mathers, *Today's Christian Woman*, January/February 2004.

"Putting on a wedding band didn't change the way I related to men."

TODAY'S CHRISTIAN

woman

REAL STORIES · REAL ISSUES · REAL FAITH

JULY/AUGUST 2005

author
SHANNON ETHRIDGE
on battling SEXUAL TEMPTATION
and finding love in all the *right* places
PAGE 28

YOU'VE GOT PRAYER! A creative approach to spiritual support

WHEN YOUR DOCTOR MAKES A MISTAKE—
How should YOU respond?

ARE YOU AND YOUR SPOUSE *SOUL* MATES?

Faraway Friends
6 secrets to staying close

HOW TO FIND THE RIGHT CHURCH HOME

IS IT A SIN TO MARRY A NON-CHRISTIAN?

Shannon Ethridge:
Finding Sexual Integrity

A uthor Shannon Ethridge admits she learned her lessons about sexual integrity the hard way. Now she's helping other women and their daughters avoid her mistakes and find love in all the right places.

You've said you graduated from the school of hard knocks in recognizing and overcoming sexual and emotional temptations. How so?

When I was twelve, some uncles made inappropriate sexual advances toward me. Then, when I was fourteen, I was raped by an eighteen-year-old acquaintance.

I never told anyone about the rape because I wasn't supposed to be alone with a boy, and my parents didn't know I had done that. I thought they'd blame me for what happened. So when my mom and dad actually let me date a year later, I didn't feel as though I had a reason to withhold sex. I went from one sexual relationship to another.

When my parents finally discovered I was sexually active, my dad was deeply disappointed in me. It created a huge rift in an already difficult relationship. My father and I didn't emotionally connect back then.

It wasn't until I got to the end of my rope that I realized what I was doing was wrong. I was living with a much older married man who had left his wife for me. But when I realized it was a deeply dysfunctional relationship, we finally broke up. It dawned on me, then, that maybe what I was looking for couldn't be found in an earthly relationship. I returned to the church and recommitted my life to Christ. That's where I met Greg. A year later we married.

Unfortunately, I didn't have much time to come to grips with my emotional baggage. I soon learned that putting on a wedding band didn't change the way I related to men. I was still so hungry for male attention that I got caught up in emotional affairs with an old boyfriend, my male aerobics instructor, a fellow youth worker, and a few others.

How do you define an emotional affair?

It's that forbidden-fruit type of relationship. You begin to go out of your way to get someone's attention, or you look to him for affirmation. You don't feel good about yourself, so when you find someone who makes you feel good, you latch onto him like a leech. That's what I began doing.

Were there any warning signs?

Sure. I felt Greg wasn't meeting my emotional needs. I began to think that my husband wasn't as spiritual as Pastor So-and-So. Or, he wasn't as cute or as romantic as my best friend's husband. With each unfair comparison, I took my husband's worth down a notch. Before long, I would lose interest in maintaining an intimate connection with my husband.

On December 16, 1995, I woke up in the middle of the night during an intense thunderstorm, sensing God was telling me someone was about to die. For two months, this fear of a loved one dying hung over me. It was nerve-racking.

Finally one night, I went to a Bible Study Fellowship meeting and slithered into the pew, tears streaming down my face. The leader had us read John 12:24: "Unless a kernel of wheat falls to the ground and dies, it remains a single seed. But if it dies, it produces many seeds." I felt like a lightning bolt had come through the stained-glass window of that church and God was saying, *It's you who has to die.*

The next day, I had lunch plans with my male aerobics instructor. Talk about a lack of boundaries! I justified the date, thinking I'd have a chance to witness to him. Instead, he witnessed to me. He told me I acted like I had a neon sign on my forehead saying I was hungry for attention. Then he said, "Do you want to know how to get that sign off? You have to die to yourself, Shannon Ethridge."

My instructor told me he was a recovering sex and love addict, and he saw the same symptoms in me that he used to have. He recommended a counselor and told me we could no longer meet. That night I told Greg every word of our conversation. He confessed that he had struggled for years to find the right words to talk to me about my relationships with other men.

In desperation I cried out to God to show me why I was so needy. That catapulted me into seeking a more intimate relationship with God and beginning intensive counseling.

As I sought God as the lover of my soul, He began healing my wounds. I recognized the extent of my sin; how I'd failed to set proper boundaries and guard against extramarital temptations.

I worked intensely on forgiving every guy who had taken advantage of me or who had allowed me to take advantage of him. Most of all, I worked on forgiving my dad. For the past decade, God has helped me work on restoring my relationship with my father. That has helped tremendously in keeping me emotionally faithful to my husband.

How is your relationship with Greg now?

Today we have a much richer relationship than we ever fathomed possible. Greg has helped me better understand God's unconditional love.

Without an intimate relationship with God, no earthly relationship will truly satisfy us. We need to get our emotional needs met first by God.

— By Jane Johnson Struck, editor of *Today's Christian Woman*.
From *Today's Christian Woman*, July/August 2005.

How to End an Affair

You've done the unthinkable; you're having an affair. Now, how do you end it? Some suggestions:

1. Tell your spouse about the affair.
2. Make a commitment to your spouse that you'll never see or talk to the lover again.
3. Write a letter to the lover ending the relationship. Pass it by your spouse for approval, then mail it.
4. Take extraordinary precautions to guarantee total separation from the lover.
5. If you and the lover are co-workers, make a job change or transfer to another location.
6. Cease all communication between you and the lover. Change your e-mail address, telephone number, cell phone number, and pager numbers.
7. Ask your spouse to monitor your voice mail, e-mail, cell-phone records, and regular mail.
8. Give your spouse a daily schedule with locations and telephone numbers to account for your time. Ask the same of your spouse so you can maintain contact with each other.
9. Make all financial decisions with your spouse, and give each other a complete account of money spent.
10. Spend leisure time with your spouse.

—Dr. Willard Harley Jr. and Dr. Jennifer Harley Chalmers,
Surviving an Affair (Revell, 1998). Used by permission.

"Michael brought anger into our marriage, and I brought a lot of hurt."

TODAY'S CHRISTIAN

woman

July-August 2005

"Why I stopped worrying about measuring up"

How to Start SPREADING the GOOD NEWS

3 Mom-tested Tips to Help Your Kids

Make Wise Entertainment Choices

What transformed STORMIE OMARTIAN from a desperate woman wanting out of her marriage to a happily married best-selling author? *see page 28*

Live on Less— and Love It!

U.S. $3.95 Canada $5.50

AOL Keyword: TodaysChristianWoman
www.TodaysChristianWoman.net

Stormie Omartian: Saving a Marriage Through Prayer

S tormie Omartian writes runaway bestseller books on prayer. She's passionate about the power of prayer because of its transforming effect on her life, lifting her from a tortured past to confident hope in Jesus Christ. Raised by a mentally ill mother who abused her, Stormie spent her childhood locked in closets trying to avoid rats. She spent her teens and twenties searching for the love and acceptance she never received at home, which led to suicide attempts, heavy alcohol and drug use, and a failed marriage. Finally a friend took her to church, where Stormie discovered unconditional love through a relationship with Jesus Christ. Even after this life-changing event, it was years before Stormie finally discovered the secret to successful living: desperate prayer and total obedience to God.

What helped you deal with your traumatic past?

My best friend since high school came to Christ three years after I did and started attending my church. Because we had similarly dysfunctional families, we understood each other's needs. We began praying together over the phone several times a week.

As I matured in faith, I knew I wanted to forgive my mother. I learned, however, that unforgiveness as deeply rooted as mine must be unraveled one layer at a time. Whenever I'd feel anger, hatred, and unforgiveness toward my mother, I had to deliberately pray, "Lord, my desire is to forgive her. Help me to forgive her completely."

Over several years of doing this, I gradually realized I no longer hated her; I felt sorry for her instead. Being in touch with the heart of God through prayer for my mother brought such forgiveness in me that when she died a few years later, I had absolutely no bad feelings toward her.

How did you learn to pray so effectively?

Through desperation and obedience. Every time I read something in the Bible about prayer, I did what it said. For example, the apostle James says we don't have because we don't ask (James 4:2), so I thought, *I might as well go ahead and ask.* But James 4:3 adds, "When you ask, you do not receive, because you ask with wrong motives."

I realized I had to be obedient to God if I expected Him to answer.

But what about when God doesn't seem to answer?

Sometimes I think God allows things to go on so our roots grow strong in Him. We have to lay down our desires and say, "Not my will, God, but yours be done." When we're burdened about something, God either will change the situation or our heart.

I used to pray all the time about my husband's anger, thinking that was something I would have to do the rest of my life. Sometimes certain prayers seem as though they never get fully answered. But Michael has become so much better, and our relationship has greatly improved over what it was before. I have learned to keep praying and not give up, because a wife's prayers for her husband are powerful.

God makes a husband and wife one. So when you pray for your husband, you essentially pray for yourself. What happens to my husband happens to me. If he has a bad day, I guarantee I'll have a bad one, too. So it's to my benefit if I pray for him to have a good day.

Is that why you started praying for Michael?

In years past, it never occurred to me to pray anything more than "protect Michael" kind of prayers. But Michael brought anger into our marriage, and I brought a lot of hurt. Whenever he was upset about something, he'd lash out at me and the kids, which would hurt me even more. After fifteen years of marriage, the verbal abuse got so bad that I couldn't take it anymore. I wanted out. I had no option but to pray a desperate prayer: "God, this situation's killing me. Everything in me wants to take the kids and leave."

After one particularly rough week, Michael went on a business trip, and my kids spent the weekend with some friends. The empty house magnified how empty I felt. So I told God, "I need answers. I'm not eating until I hear something from you." I stayed in my bed, read my Bible, prayed, journaled, and fasted. Every time I felt a hunger pang, I'd pray about Michael. I sensed God saying that instead of praying "God, make Michael more this, less that," I was to pray, "God, change me to become the person you want me to be, and change Michael to become the person *You* want him to be."

It took me hours to come to the point of saying, "Okay, God, I'll stay in the marriage and do things your way." I sobbed. I felt as though I was dying inside. But I stayed with Michael with no guarantee that our life together would change. I didn't start praying that way for Michael because I felt like it but because I wanted to obey God.

What about the married woman who suffers physical abuse?

I have zero tolerance for that. I don't advise a woman to stay and pray; I tell her to get out and get counseling. Pray from afar. The Lord *never* condones physical abuse.

What other advice do you have on prayer?

I challenge women to ask, "What could I accomplish today if I allowed God to work through me? What would I like to see?" Think of something you *want* to do beyond what you *can* do, and pray for that. Too often we underestimate prayer's power. When you understand that power, you realize you can't afford *not* to pray.

Michael and I have been married for thirty-three years now, and his anger problem has improved tremendously. I believe that prayer has made a big difference. Our children are grown and out of the house, and I see that they are not angry people. I helped them to understand that their father's anger was *his* problem, *not theirs*, and we often prayed together for him. They too see that he is so much better today.

Some day, when we get to heaven, I hope we'll see all the ways God answered our prayers even when we didn't know about it. That's why I encourage women to pray. Sometimes it feels as though our prayers aren't heard; that we're babbling into space or that our words hit the ceiling. But God hears those prayers and is responding to them.

—By Ginger E. Kolbaba, managing editor of *Marriage Partnership*.
From *Today's Christian Woman*, July/August 2002, page 28.

Power Prayers for Your Husband

Try bringing these power-packed prayers to the One who can change anyone—even you and your spouse!

1. *Pray for yourself.* Focus on loving your partner more, treating him with courtesy and compassion. As we improve our words and behavior, we pave the way for our spouse to make similar changes.

2. *Pray for your marriage.* Pray that you both will make your marriage a priority, committing time to understanding each other and placing each other's needs above your own.

3. *Pray for health.* Pray that your spouse will be able to fight minor illnesses and major diseases and that his life will be long and free from sickness.

4. *Pray about temptation.* Whether it's alcohol, food, pornography, overspending, drugs, gambling, or anything else, pray for your mate's strength to fight against temptation.

5. *Pray about work.* Pray that your spouse will find balance in his work. Pray that work will bring him a sense of fulfillment, meaning, purpose, and personal satisfaction.

6. *Pray about fears.* Pray that your partner can overcome fears about safety, finances, failure, or death. Also, pray that you can help him with reassurance and support.

7. *Pray about faith.* If your partner struggles with faith, don't preach or pressure. Instead, pray and live an example of a godly life.

—Steve Stephens, adapted from *20 Surprisingly Simple Rules and Tools for a Great Marriage* (Tyndale House, 2003). Used by permission.

"When we saw the news coverage of the Pennsylvania crash, I felt a knot in my stomach."

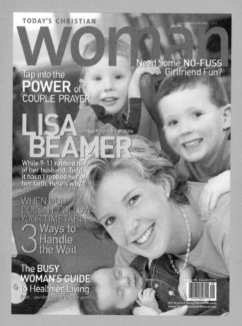

TODAY'S CHRISTIAN

woman

Tap into the
POWER of
COUPLE PRAYER

Need Some NO-FUSS
Girlfriend Fun?

LISA
BEAMER
United Flight 93 widow

While 9-11 robbed her
of her husband, Todd,
it hasn't robbed her of
her faith. Here's why.

WHEN GOD
DOESN'T FOLLOW
YOUR TIME TABLE
3 Ways to
Handle
the Wait

The BUSY
WOMAN'S GUIDE
to Healthier Living
(psst…you don't have to go to the gym!)

Lisa Beamer:
Finding Strength in Sorrow

On September 10, 2001, Lisa Beamer, age thirty-two, was an anonymous New Jersey homemaker, mother of two toddlers, David and Andrew, and pregnant with a third. Life was busy, full, and good. The next day she was front-page news.

Lisa's husband Todd was on the United plane that crashed in Shanksville, Pennsylvania, right after two jets had crashed into the World Trade Center in New York City and the Pentagon in Washington, D.C.

Todd's heroic words "Let's roll!" and actions to bring Flight 93 to ground rather than let it target another U.S. landmark thrust his wife into the national spotlight. Lisa quickly became a symbol of grace, born out of the faith that she and Todd have had since early childhood.

How do you recall what happened to you on September 11?

I vaguely remember Todd kissing me good-bye before he took off early that morning for his business trip. Being five months pregnant, I was eager for some extra sleep before the boys got up.

I was doing laundry when my friend Elaine called to tell me to turn on the television to see what was happening to the World Trade Center. When we saw the news coverage of the Pennsylvania crash,

I felt a knot in my stomach. A couple minutes later, the media said it had been a United flight from Newark to San Francisco. As soon as I heard that, I cried out "No!" and crumpled to the floor.

The week after the crash, I couldn't sleep more than an hour or so at a time. Thoughts rushed through my mind: *How can I do this? What about our baby?* I'd look out at the night sky from my bedroom windows. That enormous, star-filled sky helped me focus on the bigger picture. My own little world was a mess, but God was still who He is, and I needed to look beyond my own devastation.

That calm enabled me to get through Todd's memorial service, visit the crash site in Shanksville, head to New York for live interviews, and then fly to Washington, D.C., to attend the President's address.

Did you feel uncomfortable with so much media exposure?

At first, I didn't realize it was happening; I simply was responding to requests. But now I remind people I'm just one of many affected by the tragedy. There are three thousand other stories just as horrible as mine.

What made me feel uncomfortable was that because our family got so much attention, people sent us money and all sorts of things. So we started The Todd M. Beamer Foundation to use that money to help the families of other victims. We know that years from now, when September 11 is a distant memory for most people, the children of parents killed on Flight 93 still will be dealing with its ramifications. The foundation exists to assist those children so they'll be better equipped to move forward in life. (Note: The foundation has now become Heroic Choices, a non-profit youth services organization that builds resiliency in children who have experienced trauma. The twelve-month program supports children, families, and mentors.)

It's living with both grief and hope. I can look at a situation two ways. I can say, "Poor me," because I have to do something by myself. That's when I get swallowed by self-pity. Or I can say, "I feel relatively happy today. My kids are doing well, and I'm blessed to have them."

For example, this morning, David and Andrew flew into my bedroom in their Buzz Lightyear pajamas and Yankee hats. They pretended to be a pitcher and a catcher. They were so cute! As I lay on the bed watching them, I wished Todd were lying right next to me, and we could laugh together at the boys.

Suddenly I faced a choice: Do I wallow in self-pity because Todd isn't here? Or do I enjoy my kids? And I said to myself, "I'm going to enjoy my kids. I'm taking all of my thoughts and making them captive to Christ."

My dad died suddenly from an aneurysm when I was fifteen. I was extremely angry with God about that. It took me about five years to realize that if God had wanted to change events, He would have. He knew all the ramifications for our family, yet He allowed my father's death.

After years of wrestling with the unfairness of my father's death, a light bulb went on in my mind. I finally was able to say that while my father's death wasn't what I wanted and caused me great grief, God was a good God, and I would trust Him. When September 11 happened, I had that anchor to grab onto. I'm thankful for the wisdom that came out of my dad's death, because without it these last years would have been much different.

Our pain is so real to God. He understands it from a personal standpoint, and that's a tremendous comfort to me.

—By Jane Johnson Struck, editor of *Today's Christian Woman*. From *Today's Christian Woman*, September/October 2002.

Help for Grieving Kids

Though we can't prevent loss, here's what we can do to help our kids bear the load of grief and grow stronger because of it.

1. *Let the tears flow.* Tears are a gift from God, not a sign of weakness. It's not always our job to take away the hurt, but we can offer an empathetic, listening ear to a child in pain.

2. *Focus on their needs.* The circumstances surrounding a death, serious illness, or even a move can be confusing for children. Allow them to visit a loved one in the hospital, help plan a funeral, or make decisions about a move. That will give them a sense of control and help them cope more easily.

3. *Follow their lead.* When children are afraid or confused, they ask a lot of questions. Answer them simply, carefully, and briefly. Avoid euphemisms such as "Grandpa went to sleep." This only confuses children. Telling them half-truths interferes with their ability to believe everything else we say. But on the flipside, be careful not to share too much information.

4. *Celebrate your hope in heaven.* The Bible doesn't forbid grief; it tells us to grieve with hope. So share this hope with your children. Talk about some losses you experienced in childhood. Explain how God used the situation to help you grow.

—By Joanna Bloss. From *Christian Parenting Today*, September/October 1999.

"I was ashamed that I'd failed in the primary relationship in my life."

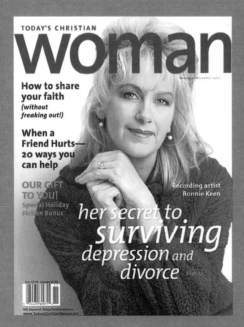

TODAY'S CHRISTIAN

woman

How to share your faith
(without freaking out!)

When a Friend Hurts—20 ways you can help

OUR GIFT TO YOU!
Special Holiday Fiction Bonus

Recording artist
Bonnie Keen

her secret to
surviving
depression *and*
divorce

U.S. $3.95   Canada $5.95

Bonnie Keen:
Digging Out of Depression

Christian singer Bonnie Keen, a member of the
contemporary Christian vocal group First Call, endured
divorce, depression, and the destruction of her career.
Here, she tells of the surprising companion she found in
her darkest hours, and reveals her secrets to survival, hope, and joy.

**When you were married, you found out your husband had
fallen in love with someone else. How did you discover that?**

Through some friends. My husband actually told them he was
in love with a woman he had met at work. I finally got him to talk
about the other relationship in counseling. We went through a
gut-wrenching year and a half of talking, counseling, and trying
everything I could think of to make our marriage work. But we didn't
make much progress.

My health rapidly deteriorated. I lost a ton of weight and
underwent two surgeries for precancerous conditions. After much
time and many health problems, I filed for divorce.

How did others respond to the divorce?

Everyone but our closest friends who knew the whole story felt
I was the villain. People who didn't know me well wrote me scathing

letters. I was already beating myself up over the whole thing, feeling I had failed God, my parents, my friends, my husband, and my children. Even though I felt God's release to move ahead with the divorce, I was ashamed that I'd failed in the primary relationship in my life.

Have you been able to forgive your ex-husband?

Yes, but it didn't happen overnight. Sometimes all I could say was, "I'm willing to forgive at some point, but I'm not there now." God used that willingness.

The reality is, there are two people involved in a divorce and two sides to every story. I needed forgiveness as much as Daniel did. Sure, technically his relationship with another woman split us up, but I wasn't perfect, either. When I realized how much God had forgiven me, I couldn't help but believe that forgiving my husband was my door to peace.

What was happening with First Call at this point?

Marty McCall and Marabeth Jordan, the other two people at First Call, were like family to me. They offered me support and stability during the divorce.

But when we went on a tour with Michael English, Michael and Marabeth spent a lot of time together. Their interactions seemed inappropriate for people who were married—and not to each other. Their flirtatious behavior really bothered me. I knew that what had happened in my own marriage must have started out the same way. I didn't want them to go through what I had, so I confronted Michael and Marabeth.

They were both very angry with me. After wrestling, praying, and talking with Marty about the situation, I decided I needed to leave the group. The night I planned to tell everyone I was leaving First Call, Marabeth finally confessed the affair to the group. Marabeth ended up leaving the group, while I stayed.

How did others respond to the affair?

Nothing like this had ever happened in the Christian music industry, and nobody knew how to respond. We were all in shock. A lot of people cancelled our concerts. A few close friends called us, and Warner Alliance offered First Call the opportunity to record two albums as a duo. But the rest of the Christian music industry disappeared for us.

I sank into a deep depression. I was crying constantly, barely sleeping two hours at a time, and unable to eat. Most days I wanted to die. Finally, in the midst of a total breakdown, I went to my pastor's office. He got me to a doctor right away who immediately put me on an antidepressant.

Were you hesitant to go on medication?

Thankfully, my pastor and my physician, who is also a Christian, had the wisdom to tell me this depression had nothing to do with my faith. But I'll admit I had to get past the thought that Christians are supposed to be happy and that depression is just a sign of weak faith.

How did you change that faulty thinking?

To be honest, at first I got angry with God. I had been through divorce, single parenting, financial struggles, the destruction of my career, and now depression. I remember lying on the floor with my Bible open on me, weeping and telling God, "I'm beginning to doubt You're there because I can't see You anywhere. You're making my life worse."

I then lashed out at God and said, "You know what? I'm sick of this. I'm either going to go deeper with You than I ever have, or I'm just turning away for good."

How did God respond?

An amazing thing happened. In the depth of my despair, I realized the only one who truly understood my pain was God. Bible stories kept coming to my mind; horrible stories of death, destruction, and despair. And I was struck that God didn't leave out parts of the Bible that are ugly or depressing. I suddenly related to those stories, realizing how God had been there in each one.

How did this hope help you recover?

At about the same time I was making these realizations, my body was stabilizing. It took me about a year to get back to normal. The medication took the edge off the utter despair and hopelessness in which I'd been trapped. And with a rested body and clearer thinking, I was finally on my way to healing.

Since then I have written *A Ladder Out of Depression* (Harvest House, 2005). First Call, the original trio, has released an album of hymns titled *Rejoice*. And, after thirteen years, Marabeth apologized to Marty, me, and other members of First Call. In the most powerful way she asked for forgiveness for all the time her affair cost us. We are at peace with her, and that is an answer to prayer.

I have learned firsthand that nothing is ever wasted if you give it to God. He has redeemed every broken place in my life. Sometimes it has taken a while to see His hand. But His redeeming power keeps me going.

—By Camerin Courtney, managing editor of *Today's Christian Woman*.
From *Today's Christian Woman*, November/December 2000.

A Checklist for Depression

Are you clinically depressed or just blue? Should you be on anti-depressant medication, or should you just tough it out? Should you be seeing a therapist, or do you just need a helpful, caring friend? Here's a checklist for guiding you to some answers.

Symptoms of depression

- Sleeping most of the time or very little
- Drastic increase or decrease in appetite
- Crying frequently for no apparent reason
- Symptoms lasting more than a couple weeks

Other possible conditions to rule out before assuming depression

- Premenstrual Syndrome
- Thyroid imbalance
- Low blood sugar
- Anemia

How Do I Find a Counselor?

Ask for a personal referral from someone you know and trust. Ideally, try to get a recommendation from someone who has seen this therapist. If you can't find someone that way, ask your doctor or pastor for a few names. Look for a licensed psychologist, social worker, or family therapist who shares your values and faith (psychiatrists typically don't do much counseling).

Consider logistics. Is this counselor covered by your insurance policy? Is the cost doable?

—Linda Eiserloh, licensed clinical social worker,
Today's Christian Woman, November/December 1999.

"I was a desperately needy woman who saw relationships with men as a way to validate my existence."

CELEBRATING 20 YEARS
Today's Christian
Woman
Mar/April 1900

The
DAY the
TWISTER Hit

Confessions
of a Rookie
MOM

Making Peace
with Your
EMOTIONS

Author
Michelle McKinney Hammond

Why She's Sassy, Single,
& Satisfied
page 42

U.S. $3.95 Canada $5.50

AOL Keyword: TCW
www.TodaysChristianWoman.net

Michelle McKinney Hammond:
Finding Satisfaction in Singleness

t's hard to believe Michelle McKinney Hammond, who is a writer, singer, speaker, art director, playwright, voice-over announcer, and co-host of the Christian television talk show *Aspiring Women*, struggled through years of unhealthy relationships in an effort to feel good about herself. Here's how the woman who almost became a Playboy Bunny now teaches women to celebrate their unique, God-given purpose in life.

You seem so self-confident now, yet you talk about feeling rejected and isolated. What happened?

I was born in London, moved to Barbados, then to America. Each place left me with a heavy accent that made me different from other children. Besides that, I was an ugly duckling with a gap between my front teeth, glasses, and an extremely thin body. My escape was spending time alone reading books. When I'd venture out, I'd try to buy friends by giving them things. I thought I could earn their approval and love, which, of course, was untrue and unhealthy.

Did those insecurities lead to bad relationship choices?

Yes. Before I became a Christian, I was a desperately needy woman who saw relationships with men as a way to validate my existence. I was also into glamour, so I thought being a Playboy Bunny would be exciting. I wanted to feel adored and in demand so I actually interviewed for the position. But while I was on the waiting list, I became a Christian and landed a job as an advertising executive.

What else changed in your life?

While I was thrilled by God's unconditional love, I was still bent on meeting my physical desires. Core attitudes like that sometimes take a long time to change. About a year and a half after I became a Christian, I became frustrated that I was still single. I got really angry with God and said, "You know, Lord, I don't want a husband until You prove I can be happy with just You. I'll never be able to tell anyone You satisfy all our needs until You prove it to me." God took me up on that. Of course, some long lonely days I regretted those words!

What happened when you made this deal with God?

Nothing changed right away. After seven years, I still hadn't received a husband and decided to take my life back into my hands. I jumped in and out of some unfulfilling relationships. Then I met the man of my dreams. When our relationship ended, I was heartsick. Even though I knew this man wasn't God's best for me, I had a hard time moving on. My pain was so intense that I physically hurt. Many days I would walk down the street fighting back tears until I got home.

Eventually I got tired of being sick and tired. One morning I told myself, "Michelle, you have a choice. You can either be happy or sad today." So I started consciously choosing happiness every day. I also said to God, "I know You love me. I know You want what's best for me. I've got to trust You to bring that about." I'd repeat that over and over until I released the pain and allowed the truth of those words to seep into my heart. I also began praying, "God, deliver the right person into my life when You know the time is best."

In the process, my perspective changed. I've found that when we single women stop asking, "Why am I alone?" and start asking God, "Why am I here?" our world changes. We start rediscovering old dreams and discover creative ideas on how to use our gifts to bless other people. Finding a mate becomes less important when we find joy and meaning because that hole in our heart isn't about a person. It's about fulfilling our God-given purpose to do what we were created to do.

So, it was an attitude shift?

Yes. My thinking changed. I started loving the people God placed in my life rather than pursuing people who weren't interested in my love. I realized I'd been squandering my time looking for a man instead of investing in my family and the rich network of friends God had already given me.

Do you still long to get married?

Before, if I met a nice guy, I'd jump at the opportunity to date him, to go for it while the getting was good. But now I understand I've been specially made to complement a certain type of man. Right now I'm happy. My life is full. I'm fueled with passion for everything I'm doing, and I think I'd be nearly overloaded if I had to be passionate about somebody else, too. So that's up to God. I'm just glad to say I've discovered single and happy can co-exist. For now, that's enough.

—By Camerin Courtney, managing editor of *Today's Christian Woman*.
From *Today's Christian Woman*, March/April 1999.

A New View of Dating

If you have viewed dating only as a search for the love of your life, here are some thoughts to help shift your thinking:

1. *See dating as a time to find out more about people.* Stop evaluating those you date by some pass-or-fail test for marriage and just get to know them. You will discover valuable things you may never have seen before.

2. *See dating as a time to learn more about yourself.* Monitor your feelings, reactions, and character as you date different kinds of people. Dating can help you figure out who you are so you will spend more time with people who are good for you.

3. *See dating as an end in itself.* If you're not having fun dating, something is wrong. You may be judging each person as potential marriage material. Instead, date to have fun. Date to learn.

4. *See dating as an opportunity to serve others.* Try viewing dating as a time to treat others well. Help someone you date see what is good in life. Find ways to love and serve that person.

5. *See dating as an opportunity to grow.* If you suspect you need to be more direct, practice that with your dates. If you need to open up and talk about yourself, your feelings, and your wants, practice that in dating. Dating is time to develop the parts of you that need spiritual growth.

—By Dr. Henry Cloud. Excerpted from *How to Get a Date Worth Keeping* (Zondervan, 2005). Used by permission.

"I knew the only way we could get through to Chrissy was through serious, intense prayer."

Carol Cymbala: Dealing with a Prodigal Child

Though it was not the path she would have chosen, the pain of a runaway daughter helped Brooklyn Tabernacle Choir's director, Carol Cymbala, discover the truth about God.

What happened with your daughter, Chrissy?

Chrissy, our eldest, had always been a model child. But when she turned fifteen, she did this about-face. She started hanging around with the wrong people, and she turned her back on the Lord. She went so far away from God that we didn't even know her. It was as if she were another human being. She wasn't the daughter I had raised.

We began sensing a hardness in her, a lack of interest in God, and a growing tendency toward deception and destructive behaviors. Her attitude was, "I'll do things my way." By the time Jim and I finally realized what was going on, it was too late. The situation culminated in her running away from home.

Did you have any contact with Chrissy after she left?

I did. Chrissy stayed in several different places. Sometimes she'd call me. Sometimes she'd communicate with a good friend of ours who'd let us know how to get in touch with her. I couldn't bear not to have contact. While the separation was extremely hard, just hearing her voice and knowing she was okay gave me some comfort. I never stopped praying for her. My prayer was that God somehow would shine His light into her heart, and that she'd be drawn back into His love.

Did you ever blame yourself?

Oh, yes. I'd think, *I'm not a good enough mother.* So naturally when Chrissy rebelled, my mind went, *Oh, I should have done this. I should have done that.*

I've now come to this understanding: Even though I haven't been the perfect parent, my children know unequivocally that Jim and I love them and would do anything within our power for them. God used that knowledge to comfort me when the guilt showed up.

So what finally happened with Chrissy?

I knew the only way we could get through to Chrissy was through serious, intense prayer. There was nothing else we could do; words with her didn't mean anything. But I knew prayer was so powerful that God could change her.

Well, one Tuesday night when Chrissy was at her worst and still away from home, Jim was leading the church's prayer meeting when a woman handed him a note. It said, "I really feel we need to pray for your daughter." After reading that note, Jim broke down in tears. He asked one of his associates to lead the church in prayer for Chrissy. About two thousand people lifted Chrissy up to God.

That very night, as Chrissy lay in bed, she had this vision of seeing herself going down into a horrible abyss. She thought, *Oh no, I'm heading toward destruction!* Hell became real to her. She cried out to God, repented of her sin, and asked God to forgive her. And He did a total overhaul on her.

Right after that, Chrissy came home and knocked on our front door. I'll never forget that moment.

She knocked on the door?

Well, she rang the bell. I opened the door and there Chrissy stood. She said, "Is Daddy here?" Jim was upstairs, shaving. I ran upstairs into the bathroom and said, "Chrissy's here." He looked at me, wiped the shaving cream off his face, and went downstairs. Chrissy was in the kitchen. Jim went into the kitchen, and she walked over to him and knelt before him. It was so beautiful.

She said, "Dad, I've sinned. I've come back to God, and I want to ask your forgiveness too. I'm so sorry." And that was it. After about two-and-a-half years of rebellion, Chrissy's life was turned around. It was like the prodigal coming home.

When I think of what God has done in her life; that's faithfulness. Chrissy has since married a wonderful man. They have three children and live in the Chicago area, where they pastor The Chicago Tabernacle.

There have been hard times in my life. There are hard times for everybody who wants to do God's will. Life's not easy. But when I look back and see how God has ordered everything, it's amazing how each piece fits. It's like a puzzle. When you're in the middle of it, you can't see the big picture. But when you look back, you see how all the pieces fell into place.

When we get through a rough time, we see how God has been truly been faithful. And how He uses everything—our heartaches and everything else—for His glory.

Look at the cover of my book, *He's Been Faithful*. There are hands lifted in worship below the title. Just knowing whose hands those are and the story behind them moves me. Those hands—my "prodigal" daughter Chrissy's hands—are lifted up to say God is faithful. And He truly is.

—by Ginger E. Kolbaba, managing editor of *Marriage Partnership*. From *Today's Christian Woman*, November/December 2001.

Coping with a Runaway Child

So what do you do when your child takes off after a major blow-up? Some tips for anxious parents:

- *Air your pain.* Do that with trustworthy confidants. While we were initially guarded about letting our problem with our daughter show, we eventually couldn't hold out. And the perspectives we gained from others were invaluable.

- *Be a parent.* One day I realized that the biggest adolescent in our household wasn't my daughter; I had abandoned the role of parent and become another teenager. I wanted so much to control the situation that I forgot my primary role as nurturer and guide. If I didn't get back to treating my daughter with respect, no matter what she did or said, the downward spiral would never end.

- *Trust God.* Never doubt that God understands. In one of my lowest moments, I heard a sermon by a friend who told about the time his daughter almost died in a car accident. As I listened, I realized how little I cared whether my daughter lived or died. "Forgive me, God, for my self-absorption," I prayed. "You created my daughter, and You're not surprised by anything she's doing. Help me to love her the way You do."

- *Take it one step at a time.* Be grateful for small blessings. We learned to give thanks whenever there was a single day without eruption. Sometimes we even broke the day down into smaller chunks. If breakfast went peacefully, we rejoiced!

—Reporting by Bob Moeller and Dean Merrill. From *Leadership*, March 7, 2002

"I'm no expert at being disabled. It's hard. It's always inconvenient."

TODAY'S CHRISTIAN

woman

REAL STORIES • REAL ISSUES • REAL FAITH!

Author and disabilities advocate
JONI EARECKSON
on the PURPOSE of suffering
and the importance
of COMMUNITY SEE PAGE 38

SHOPPING
FOR MR. RIGHT
*Is it time to chuck
your checklist?*

How Christian
"CHICK LIT" is changing
literature—*and lives*
*PLUS: TCW's new
online book club!*

4 WAYS TO HELP YOUR
OVERWEIGHT CHILD

Surviving the Scandal
ENRON Whistleblower
Sherron Watkins
Speaks Out

U.S. $3.95 Canada $5.50
www.TodaysChristianWoman.com

Joni Eareckson Tada:
Finding Purpose in Suffering

When she was age seventeen, Joni dove into shallow water, hit a rock, and became paralyzed from the neck down. Since July 1967, she has endured the physical consequences of quadriplegia: daily pain; frail bones weakened by lack of use; the danger of bladder infections, pressure sores, or a collapsed lung; and dependence on caregivers for intimate bodily functions. Here Joni talks about life in a wheelchair and the purpose of suffering.

Many people feel they never could respond to being in a wheelchair with the kind of faith you have.

I'm no expert at being disabled. It's hard. It's always inconvenient. Every morning when my girlfriend comes in with a cheery hello to get me up, I take a deep breath and think, *Here we go again.* Then I pray, "OK, Lord, show up big time. I need You, Jesus, very much today." It's a daily, hard-fought-for, desperate pulling down of grace from heaven.

It sounds as though you have great friends who help you.

My friendships go way beyond talking about what was on television yesterday. They have to, because my girlfriends apply my lip liner. They clean my catheter. They empty out the leg bag that collects my urine. I could not do what I do without my girlfriends.

Does this take some of the care-giving pressure off your husband?

Big time. I fight hard not to turn my husband, Ken, into my caregiver. I want him to be my *husband*. When it comes time for Ken to help me each evening—he gets up and turns me over in the middle of the night to avoid pressure sores—I don't want him to think, *Oh boy, one more thing.* My friends give Ken a chance to break free of the male-attendant mode. That makes me feel good, and it binds us together in a common bond of love and trust.

You've said you believe God allowed your accident. That's hard for some people to accept.

That's because God is the author of every good thing, and people wonder: *How could quadriplegia be good?* Too often we try to figure out how God might fit our circumstances into His plan for good, which *we* think will result in a new job, healing, somebody's salvation, or a husband coming to repentance. But God's driving desire is to rescue us from sin. His goal is to aid us in rooting out everything that separates us from our ultimate happiness, which is becoming more like Christ. We think happiness is found in purchasing that tennis bracelet, getting that second car, redecorating that back bedroom, or losing those extra pounds. Yet Jesus constantly tells us, "Be holy as I am holy."

Even If His way is incredibly hard?

Oh, I have the easy way. Sometimes I look at some of my friends who are struggling with obeying God, and I thank Him that because of my disability, I don't have a lot of options. I can't reach for that pleasure, or grasp at that thing I think might give me happiness. I have no choice but to look to God to meet all my needs.

In his book *A Shepherd Looks at Psalm 23*, Philip Keller, a former shepherd, explains that sometimes a shepherd needs to take his rod and splinter a certain lamb's shin so it can't keep wandering off. Before my accident, I was that wayward lamb. I was going to purchase my birth control pills, go off to college, sleep with my boyfriend, and do my own thing. Then God took His rod and splintered my shin so I would have to be carried in His arms. The cracking of my shin is a severe mercy. But look where it's landed me—in God's lap! That's a pretty nice place to be.

I don't follow a capricious God Who's caught off guard by things such as my diving accident. There's no monkey wrench in God's plan, and that encourages me.

Often Christians give pat answers to suffering.

[*Sighs.*] You have no idea what it feels like to be with people who are quick to give you sixteen biblical reasons why you're suffering. The reality is that God wants to give us His joy, but He shares His joy on *His* terms. Some of those terms call for us to suffer, as His Son did. God's goal is to make us more like Him.

I'm not saying that suffering is a really neat thing. Lamentations 3:33 says, "For [God] does not willingly bring affliction or grief to the children of men." Our suffering doesn't bring God pleasure. But I do know it means that my diving injury has potential to become a blessing. While it may have been Satan's intent to shipwreck my faith, it was God's intent to accomplish something marvelous, something grand, through it.

How do you encourage those in despair over their disability?

I first talk to their friends and their family and ask them to gather around this person to pray. Prayer is essential. We wrestle against the powers and principalities that want to use an injury or disease to cut a life short through suicide.

What helped me most after my accident, when I was in such despair, were the people who kept me committed to reality. One day my friend Jackie, who'd just gotten a yellow Camaro, visited me and said, "I'm taking you out of the hospital today for a picnic." She and my friend Connie wheeled me outside, and we went to Taco Bell. Something small like that got me reconnected to reality.

If a person's looking for a Dr. Kevorkian to end her suffering, the real answer is to mobilize community around her. Pray and then keep her connected to reality. One day becomes another day, hope builds, and hope springs eternal.

Does hope spring eternal for you?

Yes. I keep a pair of size-nine, red, high-top shoes in my art studio as a reminder of that hope. They're my dancing shoes for heaven, when I have my new body—one that won't be paralyzed.

—by Jane Johnson Struck, editor of *Today's Christian Woman*.
From *Today's Christian Woman*, September/October 2004.

Lend a Helping Hand

Millions of Americans live with disabilities that keep them from doing daily tasks most of us take for granted. Worse yet, a myriad of people suffer from diseases that go completely unnoticed; chronic illnesses, such as fibromyalgia and rheumatoid arthritis, which are not obvious but are nonetheless debilitating. If you have a friend who struggles in silence, here are some ways you could offer help:

- *At home*. Does the shower need to be scrubbed? The leaves raked? The carpet shampooed? Windows cleaned? Offer to take care of these things and others that are difficult for people with disabilities.
- *Out and about*. Offer to drive or accompany your friend to any place where she may need assistance. Arrange to get your hair cut at the same time or have the oil changed in her car during your lunch hour.
- *In the kitchen*. Offer to pick up some groceries rather than bring over a meal. Many times people with illnesses are on restrictive diets and would prefer fresh fruits and vegetables rather than casseroles or other pre-made dinners.

For more ideas and tips on what to say and what not to say to a friend with an invisible chronic illness, visit www.invisibleillness.com.

—From *Today's Christian Woman*, September/October 2006.

"It takes only a second to destroy trust in a marriage; it takes a lifetime to restore it."

TODAY'S CHRISTIAN

woman

REAL STORIES • REAL ISSUES • REAL FAITH
JANUARY/FEBRUARY 2005

LIVE with...
**KATHIE LEE
GIFFORD** She opens up
about her faith,
the power of forgiveness, and
surviving tabloid scandals PAGE 74

A Fun & Fashionable Way
to Share Your Faith

GREAT
Weight-Loss Tips
(They're painless ... we promise!)

When Your Friend
Reveals She's Had
an Abortion

How to Make
Work-from-Home
Work for YOU!

Can Your Loved Ones
See You from Heaven?

Kathie Lee Gifford: Rising Above Infidelity and Scandal

K athie Lee Gifford's life seemed an open book for those who regularly tuned in to her daily repartee on ABC as co-host with Regis Philbin on "Live with Regis and Kathie Lee" for more than ten years.

Then everything came crashing down in 1996. Despite her extensive charitable work on behalf of homeless children and AIDS and crack babies, Kathie Lee was all but tagged a child abuser when a labor-rights activist alleged that Gifford's Wal-Mart clothing line was manufactured in Honduran sweatshops. Even worse was the public scandal involving Kathie Lee's husband, Frank Gifford, after his encounter with a flight attendant in 1997. A tabloid feeding-frenzy ensued, but Kathie Lee persevered with grace under the harsh spotlights. She's no longer "Live with Regis." but she has gone live in other, meaningful ways.

What actually was your involvement in the sweatshop scandals?

I had licensed my name to Wal-Mart for a clothing line with the agreement that it would be manufactured in accordance with all the labor laws. I own no factories; I never hired a worker or went to a place where the clothing was made. So in 1996, when labor-rights activists accused me of running sweatshops in Honduras, I thought, *Excuse me? Go after the people running the factories!*

How did you handle the media uproar?

I immersed myself in God's Word. Soon after the accusations came out, I met with my accusers at Cardinal O'Connor's residence in New York City, a neutral meeting place. After the meeting, Cardinal O'Connor said, "Kathie, remember this: Our Lord did not change this world so much through His miracles as He did through His suffering. If you accept this unjust situation for His sake, imagine how you can change the world." His words transformed my perspective on suffering.

How did this new perspective affect your next step?

Believe me, I would much rather have spent time doing something different than becoming a sweatshop expert. But that's what I did in an effort to turn my pain into something positive. In the process, millions of people's lives were affected because of legislation that has been passed.

How have you forgiven those who made life miserable for you?

I learned to get on my knees and pray for those people who were saying false things about me. Luke 6:27 says, "Love your enemies, do good to those who hate you, bless those who curse you, pray for those who mistreat you." The irony is, once I've prayed for someone, I can't hate him. When you let love in, hate can't live there.

Frank is a very good man who made a very bad mistake. When Frank confessed to me in our home, at that moment every horrible thing I'd ever done flashed through my mind. And I heard God say, "I've forgiven you. You have to forgive."

I had no right to receive God's forgiveness and not offer it. So I forgave Frank. But rebuilding trust is a completely different thing . . . that we'll be doing until the day we die.

I'm no expert on how to heal a marriage. I just know the One who is. It takes only a second to destroy trust in a marriage; it takes a lifetime to restore it. I'll never be the same. I've got scars from the sweatshop thing; I've got scars from Frank's infidelity. I don't believe those scars will ever go away.

Frank came to know Christ because of what happened to us. If that's what it took to get him on his knees before God in repentance, to change his life and insure his place in eternity, then that's what it took.

Everybody goes through hard times—mine were just very public. I realized God doesn't love anybody more than He loves His Son. Yet He allowed His own Son to suffer so much on the cross. If you call yourself a believer, you're going to pay a price for it. And you'd better decide now whether you're willing to pay it.

Would I want to go through some of the things I have again? No. Would I want anybody I love to go through them? No. Would I want anybody I don't love to go through them? No. It was so awful. But so much good has come from it—so yes, it's been worth it.

—by Jane Johnson Struck editor of *Today's Christian Woman*.
From *Today's Christian Woman* January/February 2005.

Restoring Trust After an Affair

When trust in marriage is damaged by infidelity, perhaps the first question the spouse asks is: "How can I ever trust you again?"

Suspicion and disbelief move in where trust and confidence once dwelled. To begin restoring trust, the offending mate must make special efforts to reaffirm faithfulness. This means telling the spouse about activities and companions. It means finding time to be together. It means being truthful and keeping commitments.

For the betrayed spouse, rebuilding trust includes using first-person feeling statements when doubts arise, such as: "I'm still having a hard time with my doubts and fears; I want to trust you, but my anxiety sometimes pushes me into mistrust." That works better than "Where have you been? You don't care if I'm alone and worried! You've been talking to her (or him) again, haven't you?"

The first approach helps rebuild trust; the second confirms mistrust.

How can a couple move from anger to restoration? One way is to focus on your positive shared experiences. What attracted you to each other in the first place? Spend time talking about the special events you've enjoyed together, or recall the struggles you've come through together. Accent the positive to give yourself the best possible qualities to relate to. Choose the negative, and you will live with a diminished person. You will live with whichever aspect of your mate *you* choose to emphasize.

—By Louis McBurney. from *Sins of the Body* (*Christianity Today*, 1989)

"I believed we might be facing the death penalty for sharing the gospel with Afghan women."

TODAY'S CHRISTIAN

woman

November/December 2002

How to **CONFRONT A FRIEND**~
Without Losing the Friendship

Your Husband's HABITS:
When to STEP IN,
When to BACK OFF

EXCLUSIVE: **One year after their
release from a Taliban prison,**
DAYNA CURRY & HEATHER MERCER

**CAN'T WAIT
TO RETURN**
TO AFGHANISTAN. **Why they risked
sharing their faith with Muslims**~ and
why they'd **DO IT ALL OVER AGAIN.** PAGE 62

Are *You* Battling
the "Gimme Bug"?

Confessions of a Recovering
People Pleaser

plus: **SPECIAL HOLIDAY FICTION** from Liz Curtis Higgs

U.S. $3.95 · Canada $5.50

AOL Keyword: TodaysChristianWoman
www.TodaysChristianWoman.net

Dayna Curry & Heather Mercer: Finding Purpose in an Afghan Prison

After their miraculous release from a Taliban prison, relief workers Dayna Curry and Heather Mercer reveal how God revolutionized their lives, giving them a heart for the Afghan women they long to serve again.

What events led up to your captivity?

Dayna: On August 3, 2001, we were at the home of an Afghan family we had befriended. We were showing them a film of Jesus' life, death, and resurrection. I had a meeting so I left while Heather finished showing the film. Our regular taxi driver picked me up, but as we went down the dirt road, a strange man jumped in the front seat, asking, "Where's the other girl?" I refused to answer and tried to jump out of the taxi. A man from the car ahead of us, which was filled with white-turbaned Taliban, got into the back seat of our taxi. He had a whip on his lap.

I was taken to Taliban headquarters. Officials searched my purse but found nothing. "The other must have it," said one man. So they posted guards around me, then went to find Heather. They brought her back. We were locked into a cement-walled, roach-infested building, the first of three prisons that would be our home for the next three-and-a-half months. We were interrogated several times a day for nearly a month. We were treated well by our captors but were given sketchy details of the charges against us and limited access to legal counsel.

How did you respond to being held captive?

Heather: I believed we might be facing the death penalty for sharing the gospel with Afghan women, and in those moments I was not sure if I was ready to give my life for the Gospel. As days turned into weeks, then months, I began to wonder what God was doing and where He was in all of this. I did not see our prayers being answered. Physically, mentally, and emotionally I was exhausted. In my moments of despair, I started asking God, "Okay, are You here? Do You see me sitting here in prison in agony wanting to go home to my family? Do You really hear me crying every day?" I knew God was powerful enough to change our situation, but I was not sure that He would.

Dayna and the rest of the Shelter prisoners didn't struggle as much. That didn't help matters; I don't think I've ever felt so lonely in my whole life. I compared myself with them; I hated that I did not feel brave. I wanted to be strong and courageous, but my heart felt so weak and I felt so frail.

I knew something had to change. I could give God what He was asking for—total surrender—or lose my mind. By His grace I chose to trust Him. I came to appreciate and deeply identify with the words of Job, "Though You slay me, yet will I trust You" (Job 13:15). I then experienced a freedom I've never known before.

Dayna: I had peace the entire time, probably because of all the people who were praying for us. Also, six of us women would gather every morning and night for a two-hour prayer-and-worship time. We really experienced God's presence with us in those times.

George, the Shelter leader who was in the male prison, sent us a note with Psalm 118:17 to encourage us. It said, "I will not die, but live and proclaim what the Lord has done." I realized death was a very real possibility, but it seemed like God was telling us we would get out somehow. So I wanted to believe until the end that this would happen.

What I did struggle with, however, was my singleness. I turned thirty in prison and had all kinds of time to reflect on a previous relationship I had hoped would work out. Deep loneliness tugged at me. I journaled those thoughts and eventually felt God telling me, "I love you. I have good things for your life. You can trust Me." I also took comfort from the other female Shelter workers, three of whom were older than I and still single.

Why were you in Afghanistan in the first place?

Dayna: While in college at Baylor University in Waco, Texas, Jesus totally changed my life, healing me from an abortion and many other hurts. He also gave me a heart to help people. I got involved with mission work at our church and began to learn about Islam. A family from church who were relief workers in Afghanistan sent back reports of the terrible conditions there. The family asked for people to join them. Since I had a social work background, the relief organization was very interested in me. I also wanted to share the love of Jesus with women behind the veil. Heather and I became roommates during a short-term missions trip to Afghanistan in 1998.

Heather: One afternoon during that trip, our group went to an Afghan refugee camp in the city of Peshawar. Only a few fans cooled the patients in the 115-degree heat. Most of the children suffered from malnutrition. One little girl in particular caught my eye. Every bone in her body protruded against her skin. She looked like a skeleton. I watched as the little girl's mother attempted to cool her by waving a straw fan. I wondered, *How could a child ever become so emaciated?* I was moved by the injustice of her situation and prayed for the girl's healing. As soon as I left the room, I burst into tears. Nothing else in life made sense at that point except living and working among the Afghan people.

Reporters asked a lot of tough questions when you were freed about the real reason you were in Afghanistan. How did you answer them?

Dayna: I went to Afghanistan to do full-time relief work with Shelter Germany. Heather came in 2001. During my first year and a half in Kabul, I worked in a health clinic. In summer, when the women would come in and take off their burqas, they'd nearly hyperventilate from the heat. They told heartbreaking stories of lost loved ones, chronic illness, hunger, abuse from their husbands, or mistreatment by the Taliban. They tried to keep their heads up, but the pain would emerge if our conversations went deep enough. I think I helped a little by listening. I loved the Afghan women and wished for them to know better days.

Heather: We were there to serve the poor. That was our job, and we really were doing that. But personally, Jesus was the reason we chose to serve in Afghanistan. His love motivated us to serve the poor. We wanted Afghans to know that through Jesus hope was available even in the most desperate circumstances. We longed to see their physical needs met as well as the needs of their heart. Matters of faith came up daily in conversation with our Afghan friends because faith defines and influences so much of their worldview. Often women asked questions about Jesus and what it meant to follow Him. We would gladly talk about His love for them, carefully explaining that believing in Him could have dangerous consequences. We wanted them to know about the peace, hope, and eternal life that could be theirs through a relationship with Jesus. That was what we were there to do, and if that was wrong, then we were guilty as charged.

How were you finally freed?

Dayna: After September 11, 2001, we were moved to a maximum-security prison in Kabul. We experienced serious bombing day and night for a long time. When the Northern Alliance took over Kabul, the Taliban fled the area, taking us with them because they were hoping to get ransom money. They stopped in Ghazni and put us in an abandoned prison to feed us breakfast. While we were there, the city exploded in gunfire. Then things got strangely silent.

Suddenly, a man ran into our room, shouting that the Taliban had left and we were free! Men danced in the streets and women pulled back their burqas. We celebrated with the whole country.

Heather: When it appeared the U.S. Special Forces couldn't find us in the dark field, I suggested we set our head scarves on fire to attract attention. It worked; a helicopter touched down and whisked us to safety. It was a Hollywood ending and a miraculous answer to countless prayers.

—by Camerin Courtney, managing editor of *Today's Christian Woman*.
From *Today's Christian Woman*, November/December 2002.

103

Helping Hurting Women

Women of the Way empowers American women to help suffering women overseas. Using Open Doors workers in other countries and key relationships with nationals, Women of the Way delivers Bibles, children's Bibles, and Bible study materials that focus on how Jesus taught respect for the women of His day. These workers and nationals also teach literacy courses, enabling many women to read God's Word for the first time. In countries where women are unemployed or underemployed, Women of the Way teaches vocational skills.

Women of the Way has two hundred members in seven chapters throughout various U.S. cities and churches. These women are provided videos, books, a monthly newsletter full of updates and prayer requests, and ideas for raising awareness and funds for the persecuted church. As they meet, Women of the Way members focus on six goals outlined in the acronym LISTEN. You can follow these same six steps:

1. Learn more about the problem through the testimonies of persecuted women provided by Open Doors. More information on Women of the Way and Open Doors USA is available at www.opendoorsusa.org.

2. Intercede for suffering women through prayer.

3. Support countless material needs for these women. Nearly all of Women of the Way's work is funded through donations.

4. Tell others of the problem, whether your own daughters, Sunday school class, local newspaper, or politicians in Washington, D.C.

5. Encourage women of the persecuted church with letter-writing campaigns and greeting cards, which often are delivered by hand.

6. Network with other ministries to maximize their reach to women.

—By Camerin Courtney, managing editor of *Today's Christian Woman*.
From *Today's Christian Woman*, November/December 2005.

"I thought if I didn't measure up to what a good Christian woman should be, then I was nothing."

FRIENDS · FAMILY · FAITH · YOU
Today's Christian
Woman

Making Peace with Your SCALE

When a Friend COMES OUT
Now what?

I Lost My Son at Columbine
Doreen Tomlin's story

Veggie Tales'
Lisa Vischer
on accepting yourself

page 30

U.S. $3.95

Lisa Vischer: Mastering Life on a Rollercoaster

L isa Vischer is the voice of Junior Asparagus in the animated
children's video series VeggieTales. She's married to Phil Vischer,
the creator of VeggieTales. And she's mom to three children:
Shelby, Jeremy, and Sydney. But behind this apparent success
is a woman who has struggled with self-hatred and anxiety attacks.
Here Lisa talks about how she found stability on a rollercoaster ride
through life.

**You're an attractive, put-together woman. Why have you
struggled with self-hatred?**

I had such high standards for myself that I could never reach them.
I thought if I didn't measure up to what a good Christian woman
should be, then I was nothing. I couldn't seem to experience joy.
And this self-hatred eventually led to anxiety attacks.

I discovered this about myself when I went through a weight-loss
program at my church. When I stopped using food to cover pain or
fill voids in my life, I had to deal with the pain that was left. Through
daily readings and prayer, I discovered that I most feared failure.
I was afraid I could never look the way I wanted to, so I didn't even
try. I thought, *If I try, I'll fail, so I'll just stay where I am.* It was a dark,
defeated place.

God graciously brought me healing from panic disorder, but it was a long process. I sought help and counseling and worked hard to diligently watch my thoughts and take them "captive unto Christ." For example, one time I had to fly in a crop plane to reach a speaking engagement. I was afraid of a plane crash, but I knew God had called me to the task. So I brought those anxious thoughts to Christ. Into my head came the Scripture, "Not a sparrow falls to the ground apart from the Father." Instantly I was at peace. I didn't need to hear God's guarantee that I wouldn't crash; I just needed to be reminded that I am always in His hand. And that is the safest place to be.

As for self-hatred, God introduced me to the concept of grace. Although I had grown up in a Christian home and had been a believer nearly my whole life, *grace* was just a word, not a reality. I had accepted salvation but still carried the burden for every failure. Many Christians who come to Christ through grace think that they're not "good enough Christians." This is such a sad irony because we can never be good enough to save ourselves, and we'll never be good enough to make ourselves holy. We depend on God's grace for both salvation and sanctification. It's not about being good enough; it's all about grace.

How has Phil helped build you up as a person?

The greatest way that Phil helps me is by extending grace to me—the grace of acceptance combined with the grace of truth. He speaks the truth in love, which I desperately need.

Other than that, he lets me be me. One key to our marriage is that we do not attempt to fix each other but instead encourage each other to stay close to the One who is fixing us all. We are teammates running side by side in the same direction with a common goal. Marriage does not work well when we seek to serve ourselves. So we try to get out of the way and let God be in charge of each other's sanctification. This means resisting the temptation to be one another's personal Holy Spirit.

What happened with your weight-loss class? Did you lose any weight?

I lost forty pounds, began exercising, and became much healthier. These are blessings to be sure, but I try to focus more on the healing I've experienced and freedom I've received, because what God did on the outside pales in comparison.

What did you and your husband try to accomplish through VeggieTales?

As parents, Phil and I had asked, "Wouldn't it be nice if there were a trusted media company that made our jobs as parents easier and not harder?" We wanted to use the media to reintroduce biblical principles into secular pop culture.

Our thirteen-year Veggie rollercoaster ride started in 1990. Phil began creating characters, and that led to many fun, collaborative days of song-writing; recording in a cinder-block closet; writing theme songs, tag lines, scripts; and managing a small animation team working round the clock. After our first episode "Where's God When I'm Scared?" hit the market, the company and library grew quickly. The ride got faster and crazier until 2003, when it came crashing down in painful slow motion.

My greatest personal struggles come from internalizing the expectations of others. I had a hard time dealing with people who assumed we were perfect people with charmed lives. That certainly wasn't true. Meantime others sent slanderous letters to us, assuming we were self-interested and corrupt. That really hurt.

Phil and I didn't care about sales figures, money, or fame; our greatest desire was simply to "fight the good fight," yet we were becoming weaker by the day. Veggie Tales seemed to have taken on a life of its own so that the ride was now riding us! Still, we loved Big Idea and the veggies and didn't want to lose our ministry. It was a very confusing and painful time.

The two years following the bankruptcy were bittersweet; we had to process some hard emotions and deal once again with financial uncertainty. But, it was a familiar place. It actually felt like it did in the beginning; it was a much simpler time and once more we had hopes and dreams about what God might have in store. Instead of causing me to question my identity, I actually felt as if I'd found it again!

God doesn't have limited resources so He can always find another Bob and Junior. But he can't find another Phil and Lisa. I just want to abide in God's love and grace with an obedient heart.

—By Camerin J. Courtney, managing editor of *Today's Christian Woman*.
From *Today's Christian Woman*, September/October 1999.

Building Your Self-Image

Throughout childhood, we all received millions of messages from Mom, Pop, brothers, sisters, teachers, classmates, and kids next door telling us who we were. As adults we still allow those impressions to affect how we interpret life events and interact with people. If you find yourself repeating ineffective patterns in your life, this may be due to ingrained beliefs you received during childhood. Try these steps of discovery and change:

- *Write your history*. List the ideas you have about who you are: the positive, negative, and neutral messages. Try to identify where you got those ideas; who said what about you? Probably your family of origin contributed the most. Finally, identify how those beliefs about yourself have affected your perceptions of the world, and how you've coped with life experiences.

- *Check for distortion*. The most common messages that distorted your self-image pointed out some inadequacy in you. Some of those: "You stupid kid." "You'll never amount to anything!" "Can't you ever do anything right?" "You're getting fat!"

- *Reprogram*. Rethink who you are. Begin by eliminating the misperceptions. As you delete the untruths, replace them with the truth. Find Scripture verses, such as Psalm 18:16–19, John 15:15, and Romans 5:6–8, that say what God thinks about you. Recognize that your worth isn't dependent on your performance, appearance, or pedigree. You're valuable because God created you and loves you.

—Melissa and Louis McBurney, from *Marriage Partnership*, Summer 2005

"When I realized my husband could die from his illness, I suddenly understood how much I loved that man."

TODAY'S CHRISTIAN

woman

YOUR LIFE · YOUR FAITH · YOUR WORLD

SEPTEMBER/OCTOBER 2006

PATRICIA RAYBON
What she discovered about
MOUNTAIN-MOVING PRAYER
PAGE 76

**4 Ways to
Cancel *Your*
Pity Party**

SECRETS OF A
**SUPPER-SWAPPING
MOM** (and how you can be one, too!)

"The call from
United 93 changed
my life forever."

BLUE LIKE JAZZ's
Donald Miller on
**RAISING SONS
WITHOUT DADS**

3 fresh
approaches
**to women's
ministry**

US $3.95 Canada $5.50

Patricia Raybon: Moving Mountains Through Prayer

W aiting for answers to prayer can be good. But the wait was excruciating when Patricia Raybon, author of *I Told the Mountain to Move* (Tyndale House, 2006) found out her unmarried eldest daughter was pregnant, her youngest daughter had converted to Islam, and her mother, in her 80s, needed care. Meanwhile, Patricia's marriage of twenty-five years was fraught with tension, and her husband faced a life-threatening illness. Here, Patricia, who teaches journalism at the University of Colorado at Boulder and has been published in *USA Today,* the *Chicago Tribune*, and National Public Radio's *Weekend Edition*, talks candidly about finding God in failure, the freedom of forgiveness, and the ways we can move mountains in our life.

You attended church all your life, yet you say you never learned how to pray. What do you mean?

Even though I was a believer, I had become a carnal Christian. For years I prayed with wrong motives—*Grant me that job promotion!* Or, *Help us buy that house!* But the Lord says He rewards those who seek *Him*. The prayer experts say we pray, not to get, but to know God. So true prayer is less talking and more listening to God; less asking and more dwelling with God, enjoying His amazing presence. Matthew 6:33 says it beautifully: "Seek first His kingdom and His righteousness, and all these things will be given to you as well." Somehow I had never learned to first seek.

But what's the point of persistent prayer if God doesn't seem to answer?

Because, along the way of prayer, *we* change.

Recently, my best friend was praying for an old college buddy who was terminally ill. She even flew clear across country to pray over her beloved friend. A few weeks later, the college buddy died in a hospice. My friend was devastated. She was also angry at God. Why did He send her across the country in faith if He wasn't going to answer her prayer for healing? But as we talked, my friend recalled how grateful her friend was that she had traveled so far to comfort her. My friend learned the healing was in her willingness to go and be a friend.

It's the *process* of prayer that refines us. We go out in faith, and God takes care of the outcome.

But aren't we supposed to ask God for the things we want?

Well, Jesus doesn't say that! He says in John 15:7, "If you *remain* in me and my words *remain* in you, ask whatever you wish, and it will be given to you." Prayer is being in process before God. It means *keep on* asking. *Keep on* seeking. *Keep on* knocking. And our transformation is what glorifies God.

Are you saying the outcome isn't important?

What's more important than receiving what we ask for is surrendering to God. He'll add those other things that we ask for, but in His way and in His time. This kind of praying is trusting and paying attention. It means looking for answers you're not expecting.

Your marriage was strained before Dan became ill. How did prayer heal him and your marriage?

It's funny; when I realized my husband could die from his illness, I suddenly understood how much I loved that man. Talk about a wake-up call!

I'm forever grateful Dan was healed from a complicated illness. But along the way I had to learn to love him with God's love. It was hard; I studied 1 Corinthians 13 backwards and forwards, up and down. And I prayed: "Oh Lord! What is love? How does it look, feel, sound, act?" Then one day I realized love is a lifestyle. It starts with loving God, then yourself, then others as yourself. This is mountain-moving work. But the struggle and the lifestyle glorify God.

Today our marriage is better than it's ever been, but that was made possible by first seeking God in prayer.

Did you feel responsible for your children straying from the faith?

Like many moms, I confused being in church with being in Christ. For my girls, that meant going to church every Sunday, youth activities, choir, VBS, the whole nine yards. I introduced them to organized activities under the roof of a church, not to Jesus. When you know Jesus, you don't walk away from Him. So, yes, I felt responsible.

How do you pray for your daughters now?

Well, first I listen to God. Then I ask Him to show me how to pray in this situation. I never prayed like that when my daughters were little. Mostly I prayed that God would keep them safe and bless them in school—that sort of thing. Those were good prayers. But if I could go back and do it over again, I'd go for the power. I'd seek to know and follow Jesus so I could make Him known to my daughters.

While your eldest daughter has reaffirmed her Christian faith, your younger daughter is now a devout Muslim. How did you respond to her conversion?

With God's good grace. Her conversion to Islam has challenged, humbled, and even broken me. But God used that experience to help me admit I didn't know enough about Him or my faith. So I set out to learn. And the more I studied, the less I debated; and the more I trusted, the more I loved. I don't have to arm wrestle my daughter back to Jesus. I love her—and am trusting God to handle the rest.

—By Lisa Ann Cockrel, associate editor of *Today's Christian Woman*.
From *Today's Christian Woman*, September/October 2006.

What to Remember When God Is Silent

1. *Silence Is Not Absence*

God is relentlessly faithful. So how do we convince our frightened hearts of that when life crumbles around us and God becomes silent? We enter into the silence with Him. When all the racket of life stops and God's presence fills the space around us, our hearts grow calm and strong. The silence becomes an opportunity to fall in love with the person of Christ, rather than to focus on what He says or does for us.

2. *Silence Checks Our Trust Level*

Like a child learning to ride a bike, we want our parent to run alongside us, coaching us all the way. Every day God calls us to trust Him—to get out of bed and spend another day washing dishes, driving to work, and loving our family, believing He has everything under control—even when He seems silent.

3. *Silence Doesn't Mean Nothing's Happening*

Some things buried in us will surface only when we sit still long enough to let them break through. God's silence drove me deeper into His Word. I selected comforting promises, recorded them on three-by-five-inch cards, and taped them everywhere. Then I prayed the promises back to God. When I thought nothing was happening, God had me in training. I had only been interested in quick fixes. But God was building my character and making me more effective for the kingdom.

—By Verla Gillmor, author of *Reality Check: A Survival Manual for Christians in the Workplace* (Horizon Books). *From Today's Christian Woman*, March/April 2003.

"When I felt as though God had forgotten me, the question really was: What was the attitude of my heart? "

TODAY'S CHRISTIAN

woman

REAL STORIES · REAL ISSUES · REAL FAITH

Worship leader
TWILA PARIS
How she learned to live on
God's timetable. PAGE 32

NOVEMBER/DECEMBER 2005

All the juicy details
on avoiding office
GOSSIP

WHY GOD HEALS SOME
BUT NOT OTHERS

Talking Turkey
5 CREATIVE
THANKSGIVING
CELEBRATIONS

OLYMPIAN
VONETTA FLOWERS
How her faith helped
her make history

**Our Suffering
Sisters**
You can help women
of the persecuted
church *today*

**God Is My
Matchmaker?**
Your role *and* God's in
FINDING A SPOUSE

Narnia and
Your Neighbors
How a new movie
can CHANGE LIVES

Twila Paris: Finding Music in Parenting

As a songwriter and recording artist, Twila Paris has had thirty-two number-one songs and has earned ten Dove Awards and three American Songwriter Awards. She has written three books and sold millions of albums. Yet when she became a mother in her forties, she wondered if that music would fade into the past. How could she write songs when motherhood was so demanding?

What's it like to be a 40-something mother of a pre-schooler?

I was fortunate to breeze through pregnancy. But when J. P. (short for Jack Paris) was a couple weeks old, I remember thinking, "Oh, this is why you're supposed to have kids when you're young!" It's not the pregnancy that's so tough; it's the energy kids require after they're here.

The eighteen-month to three-year window was hardest for me. I had to be right on J. P.'s heels all the time, and that was exhausting. My sister Starla, who's got two toddlers of her own, once said she hadn't sat down in five years. I get that now.

When J. P. was five days old, I remember thinking, *I'll never write a song again. That chapter of my life is over.* I'd watched Starla have a baby the year before me, so I knew motherhood would consume my time. Even so, I was unprepared for the overwhelming 24/7 nature of parenthood.

But over time I learned new ways of writing songs. Instead of sitting down to write as I'd done for the past twenty-five years, I now feel as though God raises the window a crack and slips me a song every now and then. Also, with an incredible pre-school blessing running around the house, I've found worship rises up in such a natural way.

So somehow I wrote songs while driving down the road or playing at one end of the keyboard while J. P. played at the other and occasionally yelled at me to stop. I now believe even more firmly that if God calls you to do something, He'll make it possible for you to get it done.

What's your biggest parenting challenge?

J. P. is pretty strong-willed. I noticed it even before he turned one. Ironically, I'm the ultimate rule follower. If the sign says, "Keep off the grass," I'll walk on the sidewalk, no questions asked. I'm pretty structured; I have my day all planned out. Obviously a strong-willed child doesn't always cooperate with that.

How do you handle having a strong-willed child?

I was encouraged by something my father said: "Strong-willed people get things done. Your job is to get J. P.'s strong will turned towards God. Then God can use J. P. to accomplish *His* will."

J. P. has so much to learn about patience, submission, and obedience. But then I look at him and think, "Oh, God's thinking the same about me." Perhaps having children is the only way some of us can start to grasp God's heart for us, to know who we are in relation to Him, and to appreciate His infinite patience with us.

Did you ever give in to despair about not having a baby before J. P. was born?

There were many years of questions with seemingly no answers. Sometimes I gave in to doubt and self-pity. I've repented of that now. God's plan is different for all of us, and His grace is always enough if we accept it. In those seasons when I felt as though God had forgotten me, the question really was: What was the attitude of my heart in those moments? Was I reaching out for grace, or was I just fed up?

I think women who aren't married or don't have children right away can feel forgotten by God. Before we knew we'd have J. P., I thought, "My schedule's getting behind. Lord, excuse me? Over here! Everything's getting messed up."

What was God's response to your complaint about your schedule?

He didn't respond to that as much as He helped me change my prayer. I needed to come to grips with realizing that I might never have children. Thankfully, I came to a place of peace. I was finally able to say to God, "I don't have to be in control of this; You decide what's best." My prayer changed from "Please give us a baby, please give us a baby" to "Lord, please do what You know is best for all concerned."

After I discovered I was expecting J. P., I felt the Lord speak to me, "Remember that schedule? I had a schedule too, and it doesn't get behind. I do have a plan, and I haven't forgotten you."

I've learned God orders our lives in such beautiful and individual ways. Our role is to relax and learn to be content with what He's set before us for this moment with its blessings, responsibilities, challenges, or hardships and trust it's for our eternal good.

—by Camerin Courtney, managing editor of *Today's Christian Woman*.
From *Today's Christian Woman*, November/December 2005.

Relieving the Pain of Infertility

Here are some ways to comfort a friend who is having trouble getting pregnant or has just miscarried a baby.

- Give lots of hugs. Almost always, a hug is better than words.

- Write notes of encouragement. Simple notes of support after a miscarriage can mean so much. They provide an unexpected bridge between friends who have suffered similar losses.

- Acknowledge the loss. People have a tendency to avoid talking about painful things. Some fear just mentioning the loss will reignite sadness for the grieving person. The fact is people never forget their loss. Acknowledging it shows you care. Simply say, "I'm sorry you're going through this."

- Be sensitive to your friend's feelings if you become pregnant or adopt a child. If sometimes your infertile friend simply can't bear to be around you and your little bundle of joy, don't take it personally.

- Be careful about complaining. It's natural to joke about the trials and tribulations of motherhood, such as morning sickness, potty training, and all the rest. But remember, your good-natured banter might be painful to a friend who longs for a child.

—By Kathryn S. Olson. From *Today's Christian Woman*, May/June 2000.

"One of the ways I coped with Dad's problems was by being the family jester. . . . But Mother knew I laughed the hardest when I hurt the most."

CELEBRATING 20 YEARS

Today's Christian

Woman

How to
KEEP CLOSE
with faraway
friends

MARVELOUS
Moms-in-law
(really!)

**TIRED
AGAIN?**
Try these
fatigue busters

Up close with the
McCaughey
SEPTUPLETS

*Chonda
Pierce*
*Funny
Girl*

What lights up this live wire?
page 52

Chonda Pierce:
Finding Laughter in Loss

t's astonishing that comedian Chonda Pierce would feel like laughing, much less help others laugh. She grew up as a Southern preacher's kid with three siblings, one of whom was killed in a head-on car crash when Chonda was sixteen. Soon after, her father, who battled manic-depression, abandoned the ministry and left his wife and kids. Her brother married, then Chonda's other sister was diagnosed with leukemia and died. Chonda talks about her childhood, loss, and forgiveness, and the influence her mother's faith had on her.

When did you first learn your dad was manic-depressive?

I was about fourteen when I first heard the words *manic-depression*. It seemed to me that when my father took his medication or worked with a counselor to deal with his stress, he'd be okay. But then something euphoric would happen and he'd think, *I'm feeling so good, I don't need to take this stuff anymore.* After a couple months, when the medication would be completely out of his system, his mood swings would kick in. He'd become emotionally and verbally abusive to family members and to himself.

For example, he had a gun. Many nights he'd kiss us goodnight and tell us this was the night he was going to put himself out of his misery so we could all be happy.

How did you live with the terror of that?

I remember getting off the school bus and wondering what it was going to be like when I got home. Either Dad would be in a great mood and we'd all go fishing, or he'd be a basket case. Mamma, bless her heart, would be in the kitchen trying to cook his favorite meal and to do whatever she could do to pull him out of it.

If only we had fully understood Dad's illness was a physical problem. But we fell into the trap of thinking it was spiritual. Sometimes in the church there's a stigma attached to depression. We equate it with spiritual need, but sometimes depression is nothing more than a physical need, the same as if you have sugar diabetes and your body needs insulin.

How did your father's illness affect your family?

One of the ways I coped with Dad's problems was by being the family jester. I guess I felt that if I could only get Dad to laugh, or goof off, or get his mind off his problems, maybe I could fix him. When my sister Charlotta died in a car crash, I tried providing a little comic relief by boisterously objecting to God's will for our family. My humor started becoming confused, muddled.

Several months after Charlotta died, my little sister, Cheralyn died suddenly after a long battle with leukemia. After that, I became the queen of sarcasm. That was my way of dealing with it. But Mother knew I laughed the hardest when I hurt the most.

Did you ever feel as though you had to forgive God?

You know what I finally figured out? God didn't do any of those bad things to me. He didn't look down from heaven and say,

"Okay, I'm going to do this to her and that to her to mold her character." No.

Here's what happens: You get on a highway and drive a little too fast when it's rainy. And one of the laws of nature God created long before He created you or me—inertia—says that if you go sixty miles per hour and hit a puddle, you might slide into the path of an oncoming car and get killed in the collision.

God could reach down and stop that crash—and occasionally He does. But sometimes stuff just happens. When I quit blaming God for everything bad that happened, I let Him off the hook. And that let me off the hook of trying to find somebody to blame for everything.

Stuff happens. But what we do with that stuff is up to us. It's either going to destroy us, or we turn it around to help somebody coming up the road. God doesn't force us; the choice is ours.

Do you keep in touch with your father?

No, but that's okay, really. When my father divorced my mother, I didn't hear much from his side of the family ever again. That bothered me for a long time. I'm the first to admit I didn't handle my anger and frustration very well. I was an eighteen-year-old loud-mouthed, smart aleck kid, and I let everybody know it. So whatever relationship we tried to have, I did my share of making it difficult.

Did your father ever apologize for what he did?

Never. I finally got over waiting for that. Forgiving and moving on without all the loose ends tied up in a neat bow are possible only through the power of the Holy Spirit. I don't know how people do it without some professional Christian counseling.

I've chosen to remember how my dad could fix anything, how smart he was. He was personable; people loved him. Remembering the crummy stuff isn't going to do anybody any good. I want to honor my father as I honor my mother. I can honor him and praise his good qualities even when there's no word from him.

What has happened since?

A couple of years ago, I hit the wall running. It looked like I was suffering from acid reflux, sheer exhaustion, or menopause, but the diagnosis turned out to be clinical depression. Although my biggest fear and most burning question for my doctor was "Do you think I'm bipolar, like my dad?" I found the answer in a mound of understanding and compassion for my dad, a man who still lives in a very dark place.

God, our heavenly father, is the only perfect parent we know. His joy is our strength, and His love casts out all fear. With His mercy and grace, life really does go on.

How did your mother's faith influence you?

We both love people wholeheartedly. I'm so glad to have gotten that openness from her, because experiencing a loved one's death tends to make you guarded. I've never seen that guardedness in my mother. She comes out of a painful situation and dives right back into life. While we may not be alike in our clothing tastes or cooking styles, we're very much alike on an emotional and spiritual level.

—By Jane Johnson Struck, editor of *Today's Christian Woman*.
From *Today's Christian Woman*, November/December 1998.

Cultivating Joy

You'll be surprised how a little bit of discipline goes a long way toward giving you a joyful spirit. Try these action steps:

1. *Start a joy journal.* Keep a small notebook by your bed to record some good things God has done for you each day. When your heart is heavy, this may take some work. But try to come up with three items, minimum. Look back over the other days' entries to spark happy thoughts of God's faithfulness to you.

2. *Look for the silver lining.* A co-worker loathed working in our office. Day after day, her list of verbal gripes grew longer. Finally, I suggested she list what she *did* like about her job. The next day she surprised me with her list. She admitted she'd been so busy focusing on her grievances that she'd overlooked the good things.

3. *Say "thank you" before "please."* Don't jump directly into your list of wants and needs. Pray the way Jesus taught His disciples in Matthew 6:9–13, by honoring God. Your praise will naturally include thankfulness for His faithful love, the daily help of His Holy Spirit, and His provision for you.

4. *Search Scripture.* Search the Bible for God's instructions to rejoice. That will help you "consider what great things [God] has done for you." I love 1 Thessalonians 5:16–18 because it reminds me to be "joyful always" and "give thanks in all circumstances."

5. *Just ask.* When you struggle to give thanks, ask God to show you how. He's longing to give you strength for the challenges of every day. So ask for His help.

—By Annette LaPlaca. From *Today's Christian Woman*, November/December 2000.

"We had creditors calling us, and there was absolutely nothing we could do. It was just a matter of survival."

TODAY'S CHRISTIAN

woman

March/April 2002

GREAT TIPS to keep frequent-flier families CONNECTED

4 Surprising Ways GOD'S AT WORK (even when he's silent)

Need Some GIRLFRIEND TIME? Try "Project Friendship"!

Angry Moms, Damaged Kids *How to tame YOUR temper tantrums*

Devastated by debt. Then struck by a life-threatening family medical crisis. How God brought financial expert **DEBORAH McNAUGHTON**

Back from the Brink

Are You a "Hampered Chef"?!

U.S. $3.95 Canada $5.50

Back from the Brink of Financial Loss

When massive debt and a life-threatening medical crisis hit her uninsured family, financial expert Deborah McNaughton was forced to follow her own professional advice. In her greatest need, she discovered God's loving provision.

You've been a financial expert for more than twenty-five years, have written several books on credit and finances, and are founder of the Financial Victory Institute, yet nearly fourteen years ago you were $300,000 in debt. How did that happen?

In the early '90s, when the economy took a downturn, Hal and I sold two of the three real-estate franchise regions we owned and operated. Then we followed some bad advice from our accountant who suggested we sell our third region with a buy-out option.

Of course, the economy went further south and the buyer wanted his money back in cash. But we had already invested those funds in another real-estate company that never got off the ground. So we had to come up with more than $100,000.

We ended up getting loans and dealing with tax issues. Plus we had about $50,000 in credit card debt, mostly from our business, but some was also personal because we were broke.

Yes. Until that point, Hal and I were able to take care of the credit card balances each month. But our real-estate losses hit us quickly. Our incomes dropped 70 percent. Once we added all the interest on the loans, the late fees, and the surcharges, we were $300,000 in debt. We had creditors calling us, and there was absolutely nothing we could do. It was just a matter of survival.

God has always provided what we needed to survive. We never had our power turned off. We always had a place to live and food to eat. We were able to continue tithing on what little income we did have. Something always came through when we needed it, but that wasn't going to pay the loans or the credit card debt. Hal and I had created that monster.

We had created our mess. We could have blamed everyone else for it: The creditors did this; the IRS did that. But we knew we had done this to ourselves. I spent hours praying for God to give us wisdom to know how to deal with each situation that arose. I also prayed that He'd give us ideas on how to pay back what we owed.

Yes, first Hal and I decided to cancel our medical insurance. We were healthy, and insurance was an expense we just couldn't afford. Just thirty days later, the unimaginable happened. Our youngest daughter, Mindy, had to have emergency brain surgery and almost died.

What happened?

One Tuesday, Mindy complained that her head hurt. Wednesday morning she was violently ill, vomiting every ten to twenty minutes, and holding her head in pain. So after we couldn't wake her up, we rushed her to a trauma center where she was immediately prepped for a CAT scan.

The whole time I kept thinking, "We have no medical insurance. Are they going to refuse Mindy medical treatment?" But they did the CAT scan, and afterward the physician told us, "There appears to be a tumor, a blockage in her third ventricle, and fluid is filling her brain. We have a neurosurgeon coming right down. We have to get her into surgery immediately."

God's hand was on Mindy every step of the way. The surgeon said if we hadn't reacted as quickly as we had, she wouldn't have made it. He inserted a shunt in her brain to relieve the pressure and fluid.

God had healed Mindy. But then the bill came! A $50,000 medical bill in addition to our other financial problems.

So you owed $350,000 at that point?

Yes, but two miracles happened. The first was that Mindy survived the surgery. The second was that the hospital had a special program for trauma children, and Mindy qualified for it. So her bill was covered 100 percent.

In the meantime, we experienced another trauma. Hal's father had loaned us some money to pay our survival bills—house payment, utilities, food. Hal had deposited that money into our bank account. During the week that Mindy had her surgery, the IRS swooped in and took out all our money. I thought I had an arrangement with them, but I never had it in writing.

What did you do?

I called the IRS. I broke down, cried, and explained what had happened that week and how the IRS had taken money loaned to us just to survive. The woman I spoke to was sympathetic. She said, "I'll return all your money except $100." It's important to communicate with your creditors. If I hadn't called the IRS, nothing would have happened.

How did your life change from that point?

Hal decided to change careers and trained to be a financial planner. The company had group insurance—and they took us as well as Mindy.

I decided to take the advice I'd given others through my Professional Credit Counselors. Our game plan was to take bits of money, contact creditors, and negotiate with them. We finally got everything paid off, but we were in debt for about six years.

Do you think you're now better able to help other people who are encountering tough financial times?

Absolutely. If I hadn't experienced that debt, or if God had simply wiped it all away, I couldn't minister as well to others who are experiencing financial hardships.

The same goes for what happened to Mindy. God has used those experiences to help me understand the pain others feel. He's grooming us to reach out to others. Everything we go through in life is a stepping-stone to who God's perfecting us to be.

How are things going today?

Things are going great! Mindy is married and has a baby. She works with me at Financial Victory Institute (www.financialvictory.com), where we provide educational materials and counseling to individuals for money management. We also offer programs to help individuals who want to start their own credit consulting business or ministry. My other daughters, Tiffany and Christy, with their husbands and children are also healthy. It's amazing how children learn from their parents' mistakes. All my children know what not to do as a result of our mishap, and God has blessed them all.

What further lessons have you learned about managing money since climbing out of debt?

One is that the fear of repeating your mistakes never leaves. So careful attention to our finances and budget is an important way of life. Our finances are in order. An important lesson we learned about owning our businesses is not to have our eggs all in one basket. We have our money diversified through real estate investments, mutual funds, and cash.

Another is that we are more cautious about what we spend money on. We don't charge anything we can't pay back in full. We have cash reserves for emergencies and definitely have medical insurance.

—by Ginger E. Kolbaba, managing editor of *Marriage Partnership*.
From *Today's Christian Woman*, March/April 2003.

Starting Over Financially

You can make great strides this year to get out of debt. Here's how to get started:

- *Set goals that are consistent with God's Word.* Many successful people have accomplished much, yet they remain unhappy. Having singleness of purpose toward the wrong goals only leads to wrong results. So examine your motivations as well as your actions in the light of God's wisdom.

- *Ask God for guidance.* This means asking for wisdom to set the right personal priorities. God promises to guide us if we're willing to submit to Him. It's not: "Show me Your will, Lord, so I can decide if I'm willing." Rather, it's: "Before You even reveal Your will to me, Lord, the answer is yes."

- *If married, set goals together.* If you two have become "one flesh," it's critical that you have the same purpose in setting your goals. Few things will so quickly affect a couple's relationship as a financial plan that limits spending, because that will bring mutually conflicting goals into the open. If you can't agree on what your priorities should be, perhaps your marriage relationship itself needs some work.

- *Put your goals in writing, signing your name and date.* This act helps cement your thinking that you really have made a commitment of will to achieve your goals. It is also helpful to post your goals where you will see them daily to help you stay the course when you are tempted to compromise.

—By Austin Pryor. From www.soundmindinvesting.com

"My eldest daughter, Sabrina, . . . was crying, "Daddy's been shot!"

TODAY'S CHRISTIAN

woman

Why Do Guys Act the Way They Do?
(A husband's secrets revealed)

3 Great Ways to Boost Your Spiritual Life

Go to Work? Stay at Home?
Deciding what's right for *you*

Sherialyn Byrdsong
Her faith helps her turn hate around

page 20

U.S. $3.95 Canada $5.50

Sherialyn Byrdsong:
Fighting Hate with Good

While strolling with two of his three kids through his neighborhood on a balmy summer evening, Sherialyn Byrdsong's husband, Ricky, a former basketball coach for Northwestern University, was shot by Benjamin Smith, a white supremacist. Smith drove on, looking for his next victims. He killed two more people and wounded nine others before taking his own life. Sherialyn shares the pain of losing her husband and how God has helped her use this tragedy to bring an end to hate.

How did your life change on July 2, 1999?

Early that evening, Ricky asked if I wanted to take a walk with him. I said yes, but first I'd promised my teenage sister, Jocelyn, who was learning how to drive, that I'd give her a driving lesson. Jocelyn and I took the car and left for the church parking lot down the street. When we returned and were pulling into our driveway, I saw my eldest daughter, Sabrina, running down the street toward our house. She was crying, "Daddy's been shot!"

I couldn't believe my ears. We ran up the street to where Ricky was lying. He was in horrible pain, writhing and moaning.

A policewoman was already there and told me, "He's been shot in the back, but there's not much blood. He'll be okay." I believed her.

What happened at the hospital?

Shortly after I got there, my pastor and some friends came. While I was concerned about Ricky, I wasn't overly worried. I kept thinking, *He'll be okay. He'll be in recovery for a while, then he'll be good as new.*

A little after midnight, the physicians came to the waiting room. They told me they'd done all they could, but Ricky's internal organs had suffered a lot of damage from blood loss. They allowed me to go into the critical care room where Ricky was. I whispered in Ricky's ear that I loved him. Several weeks before I had memorized Ezekiel 37:9, which says, "This is what the Sovereign Lord says: 'Come from the four winds, O breath, and breathe into these slain, that they may live.'" I said to Ricky: "Live! Live!"

A nurse came into the room. She stood there a moment, then said, "He's dead, you know." I looked at her in disbelief. "Really? Dead?" She said, "Yes. Ricky's dead."

I started to sob, "NO! NO!"

How have you helped your two children who witnessed the shooting?

I made sure they went through intensive counseling. And the counselor felt their faith and what they've seen modeled in other family and church members were having a powerful impact on them. I try to remember that good *will* overcome evil.

Ricky was shot on Friday, and by Sunday we knew. People who track hate groups had Benjamin Smith on their radar screen because he'd been passing out hate literature on college campuses. So everybody started collaborating with each other. Of course, the media had been following all of Benjamin's shootings. And the police and FBI were at our house investigating.

I explained there's evil in this world, that the force behind that evil is Satan, and his spirit can incite people to kill. We talked about how some people have the wrong perspective about people of a different race or background. I explained that most hate is rooted in fear and ignorance, but that's not how we're supposed to live as Christians.

Ephesians 6:12 says that our struggle is not against flesh and blood, but against "powers of this dark world and against the spiritual forces of evil in the heavenly realms." I'm focusing on breaking down the fear and ignorance that allow hate to grow.

No. Our earthly years are temporal. I know that some day every person will get his reward, good or bad. Benjamin Smith made his decision. But whether or not he took his own life, was caught and served a life sentence, or got the death penalty; in the end it's all going to be right. It's God who determines that. He is the Just Judge.

The idea came from my former pastor, who was one of Ricky's best friends. He suggested a foundation could harness the energy of people who wanted to address the problem of racial hate. So I prayed about it and felt God leading me to be involved. Our goal for the foundation was to arrest the growing epidemic of hate and violence among youth by building their character and instilling in them a sense of purpose. We brought together youth from diverse ethnic backgrounds for different events and provided a setting where they could discuss their stereotypes, beliefs, and issues of people different from themselves. Though the foundation was dissolved in early 2006, I am continuing to work for racial reconciliation through the YWCA.

How would you like to be remembered?

I want to be remembered as being faithful to *my* course, which is raising my three children and furthering the cause of racial reconciliation. I want to be true to the call God placed on my life, so that someday God will be able to say, "Well done, good and faithful servant" (Matthew 25:21).

—by Ginger Kolbaba, managing editor of *Marriage Partnership*.
From *Today's Christian Woman*, July/August 2001.

How to Stop Stereotyping

Ethnic stereotypes on TV and in movies perpetuate ignorance between people of different color. They also fuel racial hatred. Here are ways to break the negative cycle of stereotypes in our culture.

1. *Turn it off.* Refuse to watch TV shows or movies that are needlessly hurtful to one race or another. Turn off music with offensive lyrics.

2. *Talk about stereotypes.* When you hear or see something that seems to be racially damaging or confuses you, mention it to people you trust. Ask if they heard it the same way. Don't just let the matter slide. Talking about what we hear keeps it from silently reinforcing ugly stereotypes in our minds.

3. *Make a zero-tolerance policy for your own mouth.* Refuse to tell any jokes or stories that are hurtful or disrespectful to any race. When others tell such jokes, politely resist the temptation to laugh. You could also ask, "What did you mean by that?"

4. *Get to know other cultures.* You can research and learn about other races and nations, but don't let your knowledge of other people stop with what's in books or TV shows. Talk to and build friendships with people of other races. Be open to getting to know God's children based on who they are—and not only on the color of their skin.

—By Mark Matlock, founder of WisdomWorks Ministries (www.planetwisdom.com). From *Campus Life*, March/April 2005

"I'm ashamed to admit I was full of fear and prejudice."

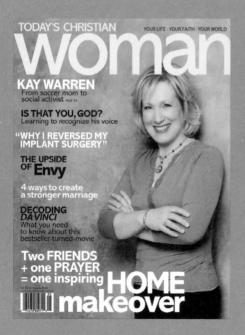

TODAY'S CHRISTIAN
YOUR LIFE · YOUR FAITH · YOUR WORLD
woman

KAY WARREN
From soccer mom to
social activist PAGE 54

IS THAT YOU, GOD?
Learning to recognize his voice

"WHY I REVERSED MY IMPLANT SURGERY"

THE UPSIDE
OF **Envy**

4 ways to create a stronger marriage

DECODING DA VINCI
What you need
to know about this
bestseller-turned-movie

**Two FRIENDS
+ one PRAYER
= one inspiring HOME
makeover**

Kay Warren: Offering Hope to People with AIDS

As wife of Rick Warren, author of the bestselling book *The Purpose-Driven Life*, Kay was a busy "soccer mom" of three. Then one day Kay picked up a news magazine and was stunned by an article on AIDS. When she read that twelve million children were orphaned in Africa due to AIDS, she realized she didn't know a single orphan, much less anyone with AIDS. Here she talks about how she got involved.

Did you ever wonder if you could even make a dent in an issue as big as AIDS?

Of course. But the day I read that article on Africa, the Lord and I began this internal dialogue. I thought, *This just can't be true. Because if it is, then I have to do something about it. But there's nothing I can do!*

I sensed I couldn't face God when He asked me, "What did you do about those twelve million children I told you about?" How could I possibly respond, "Oh, that was so sad—but I had so many other good things to do. I'm really sorry I wasn't able to get around to that. I hope that's OK?"

What did you start doing?

I began reading, watching videos, and talking to anybody who knew anything about HIV. After eight months of research, I needed more. God captured my heart through Africa, so I wanted to go to Africa.

What did you learn on that first visit?

Nothing in American life prepared me for rural Africa. Nothing. Even the poorest of the poor here have it much better than most people living in the rest of the world.

One of the first women I met was Joana. She was stick thin, plagued by unrelenting diarrhea, left homeless under a tree, and dying of AIDS. Joana was so weak that she couldn't even crawl over to greet me. So her aunt scooped her up and placed her on a piece of plastic in front of me. I couldn't tell Joana she would be healed or that I could give her a roof over her head. But I could offer her my presence, and by my presence, the presence of Jesus. And I could offer her the hope of heaven. I will never, ever forget Joana. That's why her picture hangs in my office. For me, AIDS wears a face. It's Joana's.

What happened after you returned?

God quickly showed me my hypocrisy; I cared about people far away but not for the HIV-positive people in my own church. I'm ashamed to admit I was full of fear and prejudice. I had to overcome several myths, including the one that AIDS in America was a gay man's disease.

But what if AIDS were only a gay disease? There are innocent victims of HIV—a baby born to an HIV-positive mother, a woman infected by her spouse—as well as the perpetrators—a gay man, an unfaithful husband. Why does a woman infected by an unfaithful spouse seem more deserving of love and compassion than a gay man or the unfaithful husband? Why does one seem more deserving of love and compassion than the other?

What kind of response have you had from HIV/AIDS sufferers in your community?

At the end of our first Disturbing Voices conference, we invited those with HIV to come to the platform so they could experience the repentance and love they'd never felt before from the church. About thirty people came up. As I led them toward the stage one by one, their entire bodies shook with sobs. For the next hour, conferees hugged them, prayed with them, and asked them for forgiveness.

So many told me, "I never thought this day would come. I never thought God could redeem my brokenness. I never thought anybody who was HIV-negative would care for me."

It says something that they're not used to such love.

Yes. Not long ago I met with an HIV-positive gay man, the head of one of the local AIDS service organizations, to explain how we're reaching out to his community. He tried to ferret out what I thought about homosexuality.

Instead, I told him, "I'm not HIV-positive, so I don't know what that's like. But I've had breast cancer, so I do know what it's like to have a life-threatening illness, to have to take medicine that made me violently ill, to not know the outcome of my life. But I've looked death in the face, and I'm not afraid to die."

With tears in his eyes, he said, "I'm not afraid to die, either. I just don't want to die alone." I told him I didn't believe homosexual practice was God's plan for human sexuality. This man may never believe what the Bible teaches about homosexuality, but I can't control that. What I can control is how I treat him. And when I share my beliefs with him, he'll know it's coming from someone who truly cares.

What are you most passionate about?

Believers leading the way in love. How will people know Jesus loves them unless we show up for needy people in love? And the truth is, whoever loves them first wins them.

How can women start "showing up"?

Start with repentance. I had to repent of my enormous apathy. If you don't feel called to reach out to HIV-positive people in your community, beg God to open your eyes to those who are poor, sick, or homeless. Once you do, the suffering of others becomes personal. And when it becomes personal, you start caring.

—By Jane Johnson Struck, editor of *Today's Christian Woman*.
From *Today's Christian Woman*, May/June 2006.

You Can Impact Your World

Think one woman can't make a positive impact on the world? Check out some of the ways.

- *Advocate for kids.* Help abused or neglected kids by becoming a Court Appointed Special Advocate (www.nationalcasa.org) to review cases and recommend to the court what you believe is best for these children (no legal expertise required).

- *Make money for missions.* After cleaning out your closets, attic, or basement, hold a garage sale to get rid of your extras. Donate the money you make to your church's mission fund or to your favorite charity.

- *Read to little ones.* Read stories aloud to underprivileged kids in schools and community centers one hour a week through Rolling Readers USA (www.rollingreaders.org).

- *Help someone financially.* Send an anonymous donation to a neighbor or church member who's unemployed. Gift cards to a local supermarket are a great way to help a needy family. Or check to see if your church has a benevolence fund for families in need, and support that.

- *Volunteer.* Go to www.volunteermatch.org for more ideas on how to make a difference in your community.

—By Camerin Courtney, managing editor of *Today's Christian Woman*. From *Today's Christian Woman*, September/October 2003.

"I'd be a liar to say I don't go through times of feeling abandoned."

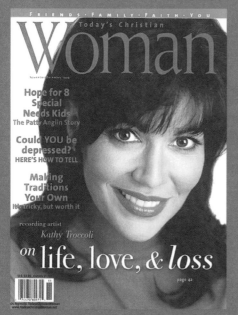

FRIENDS · FAMILY · FAITH · YOU

Today's Christian

Woman

November/December 1999

Hope for 8 Special Needs Kids
The Patty Anglin Story

Could YOU be depressed?
HERE'S HOW TO TELL

Making Traditions Your Own
It's tricky, but worth it

recording artist
Kathy Troccoli

on life, love, & loss

page 42

Kathy Troccoli: Growing Closer to God Through Grief

Dove-award winning recording artist Kathy Troccoli lost her father to colon cancer when she was age fifteen. Then, in 1991, her mom died of breast cancer weeks before one of Kathy's albums hit store racks. In 1999, Kathy's much-loved aunt succumbed to breast cancer. Despite these personal setbacks, Kathy's career has continued to soar. Here, Kathy, who calls herself "contentedly single," tells what she's learned about life, loss, love, and, most important, faith.

Holidays are such a family time. Is it especially hard for you to celebrate those with your parents gone?

I feel as though I'm a paradox. I'm such a social person, so I can really enjoy the holidays, but my capacity to feel deeply also can cause me to feel orphaned. My friends often say, "Kath, life seems messy to you because you live it passionately. You have to find a balance."

I'm trying to find that balance. But I have to admit, when it's all said and done, I've had some nights when I've experienced a lonely ache. Or I've hit the pillow longing to belong to someone.

How do you deal with that loneliness?

I remember that God says He's a Father to the fatherless. I'd be a liar to say I don't go through times of feeling abandoned, but I also know there's never been a time in my life when He hasn't provided for me, even when my dad died, then my mom, and now my aunt.

So during these times, I focus on what God says and what I've been given, because when I focus on that, all the other stuff fades. That's what keeps my head up and helps me say, "Okay, God, I believe in You. Your promises are true."

Did you and your mom always get along?

I went through a normal teenage rebellion. Yet at the same time, I wanted Mom's approval so badly! It's like you say, "I don't care what you think," but inside you're thinking, *Oh, I hope she likes what I have on.*

There were times when I'd have a date, and before I left my mother would kiss me good-bye and whisper in my ear, "He's not for you. Have a good time." Great! I'd be sitting with him at dinner thinking, *There's no way I'm going on a second date with this guy.* Mom affected me so deeply. I laugh at it now, but back then I'd get bitter about it.

How do you relinquish bitterness?

It's a process. The more you work on yourself and the more you relinquish that stuff to God, the more your response changes because there's a lot less poison in your heart.

I'm not saying I'd be totally different if Mom was alive now, but I think I'd have a different response. If I had been who I am now and she had said, "I don't like that shirt on you," I think I'd say, "Well, Mom, you know what? I love it. How about some lunch?" then move on.

The more I put things through a "Jesus grid," thinking about how He would respond in the situation, the less I react with my gut.

What are some of the biggest struggles you and other women face?

One is self-esteem. I think if every woman was affirmed in some way and told she was beautiful every day, she'd live a healthier life.

The second is that women have trouble getting their emotional needs met. They often feel empty or misunderstood. I've also learned through my married friends that a woman and a man offer two different things. So healthy friendships with other women can offer the encouragement and understanding that sometimes a man can't.

God should be enough, but we still need flesh and blood, don't we?

Yes, I think that's why women's conferences are blazing all over the nation. Some of the women who come to those conferences are overwhelmed by life. But once they're there, they realize, *I'm not the only one. God has helped them, and God is going to help me. I believe I can make it.* There's camaraderie.

You don't feel alone?

Right. We're such emotional, relational beings, but we're often ruled more by our emotions than by reason, especially if we don't balance that with God's truth.

On the days I'm feeling down, I ask myself: "Am I still lovely in God's sight even when I don't feel lovely?" Absolutely, because God tells me I am. "Is He by my side even when I don't feel Him there?"

Definitely, because He's told me He's as close as my next breath. "Does God see that I'm weeping every ounce of moisture out of my body today?" His Word says He holds my tears in a bottle.

The problem for many women is that they put God on the sidelines, and whatever they're feeling that day or week gets elevated. You're thinking, *What am I going to do with this feeling?* instead of asking God, "Help me to see past this feeling to the truth of Who You are."

Because life is messy, it's important to keep our relationship with God fresh and intimate and to surround ourselves with substantial Christian friends who know and stand firm on the Bible's promises. Those two things help me on my journey and, in the last few years, have helped me to be more confident than ever before.

What are your goals for the future?

I have been blessed; I love what I do. Sometimes the travel gets to me. I wish I could do concerts and conferences via satellite from my living room. I have been speaking and singing to thousands of women every year. I continue to see women meeting God, being healed, and given courage to get through this crazy life. I have been producing my own CDs and I am being asked to do more and more TV hosting, which has been a goal of mine. Who says life doesn't begin at 40!

—by Jane Johnson Struck, editor of *Today's Christian Woman*.
From *Today's Christian Woman*, November/December 1999.

What's So Great About Being Single?

There are many reasons why being single is great. Here are some of them:

1. *Freedom.* Freedom has allowed Karen, a middle-school teacher, to spend her summers at a day camp for inner-city kids. It has allowed me to visit my friend Christa in Germany and travel through Europe without worrying about a husband or kids.

2. *Guy friends.* Without guy friends like Ray and Max, my lack of a husband or boyfriend could be more pronounced. If I were married, I'm not sure I'd continue those friendships. I certainly know we wouldn't be as close as we are. So for now, I'm enjoying my guy friends.

3. *Time alone.* I lived alone for eight months after college. What could have been the loneliest time of my life turned out to be most rewarding. I would pray out loud while washing dishes, sing along with the radio without apology, or settle into a chair with a good book and read for hours. I wouldn't have traded that richness for anything.

4. *Our gang.* My roommate and I have three other friends in Our Gang. These friends will give me a ride to the airport at 6:00 a.m. on a Saturday morning, or bring their own slippers when they come over for movie night. I'm thankful for these God-given friends.

—Camerin Courtney, managing editor of *Today's Christian Woman*.
From *Today's Christian Woman*, September/October 1998.

"It took me a while to fully understand that depression was a medical condition I couldn't pull myself out of."

TODAY'S CHRISTIAN

woman

MARY BETH CHAPMAN PAGE 42

Surprised by
HOPE & HEALING
during her struggle
with **DEPRESSION**

Mary Beth, wife of
Christian recording artist
Steven Curtis Chapman,
with adopted daughter
Stevey Joy

Wedded BLISS!
5 Reasons to Love
Being Married

CHRISTMAS CHIC
from TV's *Trading Spaces*

"I Didn't Want to
Give Up Smoking"

Surrendering
to GOD'S PLAN
Even When It Hurts

**HOW TO
BE MORE
HOSPITABLE**
(no dusting required!)

Mary Beth Chapman:
From Depression to Daily Joy

Mary Beth Chapman never dreamed she'd travel to China to adopt three little girls with her husband, veteran Christian musician Steven Curtis Chapman, or that they'd help her in her journey toward healing from depression. Here, she talks about the surprising way God has brought joy back into her life.

Why were you initially hesitant about adopting?

For years I was supportive of the *concept* of adoption. Steven and I had prayed for and financially supported friends who adopted kids. But I feared I wouldn't have enough love for a child who wasn't biologically mine.

What changed your mind?

Several years ago, when our daughter Emily was eleven, we went to Haiti with Compassion International. After spending time with the children there and seeing how many of them needed loving families, Emily got the idea that we had room at our table for more. She talked constantly about international adoption. Emily's been intense from the womb, so her passion didn't surprise us. But when her campaign continued for two years, we wondered if God was trying to tell us something.

What prompted the final decision?

Steven and I took a day to talk and pray about adoption. At one point, Steven said, "This is a hilarious thing we're considering. If we do end up adopting, we need to find out what the word in Chinese is for *laughter*. That word needs to be part of her name because we're like Sarah and Abraham, laughing at the idea of having a baby because we feel too old."

That afternoon, Steven flipped through an eight-month-old issue of *Reader's Digest* and suddenly burst out, "Oh, my goodness!" He handed me the article he'd been reading about a Chinese boy. Right there in black and white it said, "The little boy's name is Shaohan (*shao* in Chinese means laughter)." At that point, there were just too many coincidences for us to avoid God's nudging. The question changed from "Are we going to adopt?" to "*When* are we going to adopt?"

What did you think when you first held Shaohannah?

From the first moment, I loved this child desperately and would have died for her even though she'd done absolutely nothing to earn my love. Even though I had been a Christian since I was nine, it didn't hit me until that day, *that's how much God loves us.*

How did Shaohannah handle the transition into your family?

She was a happy baby during the day, but she'd scream every night. We finally realized she had night terrors, which were her reaction to the loneliness and negative conditions in the orphanage. Those terrors continued for the first six months we had her. It took a long time for her to allow us to comfort her, to realize she was in a safe, loving place.

When did you realize you wanted to adopt again?

Practically from the moment Shaohannah was placed in my arms. Steven, however, felt the exact opposite. He loves Shaoey deeply but saw how much energy she required from our whole family with her nightly screaming and rambunctious personality. Then God spoke to Steven during a church service in which some friends of ours dedicated several kids they had adopted. Once he felt adopting another child was God's will for our family, Steven was completely on board.

When were you diagnosed with depression?

Early in 1991. Will was a newborn, Caleb was age one, and Emily was finishing preschool. Steven was getting ready to embark on The Great Adventure Tour, and we were building a home. In the middle of all that, I had to have emergency gall bladder surgery, and Steven's parents divorced.

Obviously we were under a lot of stress. I basically had a breakdown. I was extremely fearful and hopeless and couldn't seem to pull myself out of it. I was physically and emotionally depleted. Steven almost pulled the plug on the tour. Thankfully, his manager knew a great Christian counselor who helped me realize I was battling clinical depression and had been for some time. Through working with him, we realized medication was the best course for me.

How did you feel about this diagnosis?

To be honest, a bit guilty. I kept telling myself I had no reason to be depressed. I have a wonderful husband and great kids. It took me a while to fully understand that depression was a medical condition I couldn't pull myself out of or pray out of. I needed help. And with medication and counseling, I got it.

Did your depression affect your marriage?

Sure. Before the diagnosis, things were tough. I would get so explosive and often would take it out on Steven. The diagnosis of depression actually drew us closer, because we knew the problem wasn't either of us but this outside thing we could tackle together.

In the long run, God has used this struggle to bring me closer to Him. In those lonely, down times, I realized Christ was all I had. I couldn't fix myself, neither could my husband or kids or friends. Only God. And He's used our family to step out in faith and obedience to do something that looked a little crazy, to pour out untold blessings and riches in the form of these little people, who truly are the hidden treasures He refers to in Isaiah 45:3.

Now, every morning when I get up and see the smiling faces of Shaoey, Stevey Joy, and Maria, I'm reminded of the lengths to which God went to bring them into a loving Christian family. It reminds me of what He did to bring us all into His family. And it's the best reason in the world to get up and face the day with joy.

I am also helping orphans through Shaohannah's Hope, a foundation that I co-founded and lead. Our purpose is to engage churches to help Christian families reduce the financial barrier to adoption. For more information visit, www.ShaohannahsHope.org.

—by Camerin Courtney, managing editor of *Today's Christian Woman*.
From *Today's Christian Woman*, November/December 2003.

The Adoption Option

If you've ever had an inkling God is leading you to become an adoptive parent or to support a family trying to adopt here are some ways to check it out.

1. *Learn about adopting a child.* Approximately 20,000 U. S.-born infants are placed for adoption each year—as many or more than the number of international adoptions yearly. So says AdoptiveFamilies.com. On average it takes between one to two years to complete an adoption. If you're thinking about adopting a child, check out www.adoption.com. This excellent website provides information on nearly every aspect of adoption, from the legal issues involved to preparing for the new child's arrival. A wealth of information is also available on www.adoptivefamilies.com.

2. *Support adoptive families.* For many families, the biggest adoption hurdle to overcome is the cost. International adoptions can cost families upwards of $25,000. But don't let the cost scare you. For most families, adoption is often no more expensive than giving birth, especially when factoring in tax credits and employers benefits. To help families deal with the expense of adoption, Steven Curtis and Mary Beth Chapman have developed Shaohannah's Hope Foundation, which offers financial assistance for qualified adoptive families. Visit www.shaohannahshope.org for more information on how you can get involved.

—Carla Barnhill, editor of *Christian Parenting Today* magazine.
From *Christian Parenting Today*, Winter 2004.

"I didn't feel bad about being nasty on stage because the joy I felt from performing filled me up."

TODAY'S CHRISTIAN

woman

Real life hasn't always been a laugh for sitcom actress/Christian comedian

SHERRI SHEPHERD
Find out why. PAGE 37

8 SUPER SINGLES
Gutsy Gals Share
Their Solo Adventures

The BUSY Woman's
Guide to PRAYER

PAMPER YOURSELF!
7 simple ways to
relax & refresh

A Coffee Shop
That Perks Up
Body *and* Soul

BEFRIENDING
the Muslim
Next Door

Actor
MEL GIBSON
on his new film,
*The Passion
of the Christ*

Sherri Shepherd: Making Life Changes with God's Direction

After comedian and actor Sherri Shepherd turned her life over to Christ in 1993, her magnetic personality and saucy humor landed her roles on sitcoms that included NBC's *Suddenly Susan*, CBS's *Everybody Loves Raymond*, and ABC's *Less Than Perfect*. Yet being a believer in the entertainment industry is tough. Here Sherri tells about her tumultuous spiritual journey as an actor.

Did you always have the acting bug?

I think I was four when I decided I wanted to be famous. I would sing in our living room. I loved to entertain. I made people laugh. All my report cards said, "Sherri's an incredible student, but she's a class clown." When we moved out of Chicago to a suburb to escape gang violence, there weren't many black people there. We were called "niggers" a lot. I made jokes out of whatever they said. I dealt with pain through humor.

What kind of pain?

Besides the racial insults, things were tough at home. My dad was a Christian, but my mom became a Jehovah's Witness when I was about seven. To keep the peace, my father became a Witness, but he was miserable. When he questioned things, the elders excommunicated him and told us we couldn't talk to him anymore.

My mom filed for divorce, packed us up, and moved us to California. I became sexually active and got into an abusive relationship. When I tried to break up with the guy, he would follow me when I got off the bus. I was scared, but it never occurred to me to seek God. I believed God had turned His back on me.

I did my first stand-up act at an open-mike night. It was the scariest but most amazing experience. People wiped tears of laughter from their eyes because of what I talked about. I felt as though I'd come home. After that, I couldn't stop.

Was your comedy act vulgar?

It was nasty. Actor Eddie Murphy was big at the time, and he was really dirty, so I thought I had to be the female Eddie Murphy. I didn't feel bad about being nasty on stage because the joy I felt from performing filled me up.

How did you become a Christian?

I got to know some Christian comics. Their lifestyle was so different! They never condemned me for the stuff I did, but they were always there for me. I'd call up my friend Lydia and say, "Could you just think about me?" I never once asked, "*Pray* for me," but she would anyway. At one point, my life was so messed up, I was on my knees crying and praying, "I'm hurting. Please send somebody to help me."

Two weeks later, I met this guy on a bus. We starting talking, and I thought, *He's so nice, I'd like to have sex with him.* To my surprise, he asked me, "What's your relationship with Jesus?"

I lied and told him I went to a certain church. As it turned out, he went to that church. We started dating, but we remained celibate. He dragged me to church and talked to me about Jesus all the time.

What made you finally surrender?

There was so much junk going on in my life, I couldn't take it anymore. My mom was dying from complications of diabetes, and I was tired of the politics of stand-up comedy. So here I was at church, crying, "I don't know what to do." When the pastor asked if anyone wanted to accept Christ, I walked down the aisle, sobbing.

Did you clean up your comedy act right away?

Nope. One day my boyfriend said, "You don't have to be dirty," and I flew off the handle. I said, "Don't tell me what I got to do. This is what people want." He replied, "Do you think you're glorifying God?" I sat on my apartment floor, crying and praying, "Lord, are You telling me if I give this up You'll give me something better?" I felt God say, *Trust Me and see.*

I didn't clean my act up all at once, but I began toning it down. I replaced certain jokes. I stopped cursing. I wasn't always perfect, but those were the times I drove home crying because I was sorry I'd disappointed the Lord. It took me four years to fully clean up my act.

Where do you hope to be in five years?

I'd love to do films that impact people powerfully. And I want to meld my faith with my comedy. My dear friend and fellow comedian Chonda Pierce is helping me do that. I tell her my new jokes before I share them with an audience, because I don't want to be a stumbling block for anybody. I think God has an amazing sense of humor. I can picture Jesus laughing with His close friends and disciples. I thank God for the healing gift of laughter.

—by Jane Johnson Struck, editor of *Today's Christian Woman*.
From *Today's Christian Woman*, March/April 2004.

Steps Toward Change

As Christians, we become sanctified over time, not all at once the moment we accept Christ into our life. Although the changes we long for may not come overnight, here are some constructive steps you can do to keep moving forward:

• Change comes when we choose to renew our minds through hearing and reading the Word. In Romans 12:2, Paul warns us, "Do not conform any longer to the pattern of this world, but be transformed by the renewing of your mind." So don't let the world squeeze you into its mold. Our metamorphosis begins on the inside with new affections, new desires, new abilities, and a new sensitivity to sin. Eventually, these inner changes become obvious on the outside, and the change is complete.

• If we hope to make our devotion to Jesus pure and simple, we must personally read the Word. Consider purchasing a copy of *The International Inductive Study Bible* (Harvest House), and start taking apart each book of the Bible on your own according to the instructions given at the beginning of each book.

• Write down what you want to change and why. Is what you're hoping to change necessary for God's purpose, or are you instead conforming to man's image?

—By Kay Arthur. Excerpted from *Can a Busy Christian Develop Her Spiritual Life?* (Bethany House Publishers, 1994). CTI copyright.

"Because of the rape, I felt like damaged goods. I wondered if others would ever find me valuable again."

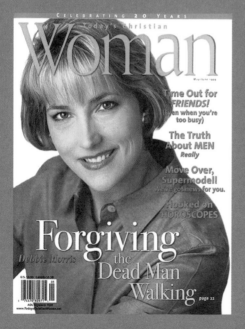

CELEBRATING 20 YEARS
Today's Christian

Woman
May/June 1998

Time Out for FRIENDS!
(even when you're too busy)

The Truth About MEN
Really

Move Over, Supermodel!
We've got news for you.

Hooked on HOROSCOPES

Forgiving
Debbie Morris
the Dead Man Walking
page 22

US $3.95 Canada $5.50

www.TodaysChristianWoman.net

Debbie Morris:
Learning to Forgive

D ebbie Morris was sixteen when she and her boyfriend, Mark Brewster, who were sitting in their parked car drinking milkshakes, were abducted at gunpoint by Robert Willie and Joe Vaccaro. Several hours later, Mark was led into woods near the Alabama state line, where he was tortured, shot, slashed, and left for dead.

For thirty hours, Debbie was repeatedly raped by her captors. Throughout that time, she also picked up some chilling clues that led her to believe her rapists had brutally murdered a young woman, Faith Hathaway, several days before.

The Hathaway murder was replayed in the 1995 award-winning movie, *Dead Man Walking*. Faith was killed, but Debbie, miraculously, was released. Her survival enabled authorities to save Mark's life. Her testimony enabled the state of Louisiana to put an end to Robert Willie's life and sentence Joe Vaccarro to life imprisonment. Here Debbie tackles questions about God's grace and power over evil.

How did this trauma affect your faith?

People told me it was a miracle that I survived. I thought if God really saved me, why did He let me go through the whole horrible experience in the first place? I was angry with God; I felt abandoned.

I tried to be strong for Mark. I felt guilty for the physical suffering he had endured while I had escaped. I visited Mark, drove him to his physical therapy, coached him with his speech. Eventually I told Mark I needed a break; I couldn't come over anymore. I felt incredibly selfish and guiltier about that than I ever remembered feeling.

Through the next several years of trials (including testifying in front of a mocking, leering Robert Willie), I convinced everyone I was fine. But I wasn't.

What toll did the rape take on you?

Not only did it rob me of something sacred that should have been mine to give away; it also robbed me of self-worth, confidence, and security—the very things you depend on to live a normal life. For thirty hours, I had lost total control of my body and my life, and I was angry about it. But I didn't want to acknowledge that anger.

Did your fear and anger lessen when Robert Willie was executed?

Not really. Mostly I felt numb. I had trouble sleeping; the thought of someone dying who hated me so much troubled me. But I realized it might be just as bad for him to die with me hating him. I knew I needed to do something to get rid of my pain, anger, and shame.

The night of his execution, as I lay in bed in the dark, I told God I forgave Robert Willie. After that prayer, I felt a burden lift. But I didn't realize I still needed to forgive others for other reasons and at a deeper level. Forgiving Robert Willie didn't bring the closure I expected. The thing I thought I'd fixed still wasn't. And that led me to a lot of poor choices.

Because of the rape, I felt like damaged goods. I wondered if others would ever find me valuable again. I didn't place importance on virginity anymore; that choice had been taken away from me.

I also suffered from depression. I lashed out at family members and started drinking to dull the pain. When I drank, I didn't feel as fearful. Finally, at age twenty-four, I checked myself into a thirty-day treatment program in a Baton Rouge hospital. There I was told I was full of suppressed anger and resentment.

After treatment, I discovered it had been easier for me to forgive Robert Willie than to forgive my mother and God.

Why were you angry at your mom?

I've never doubted my mom loved me. But I'd always had a problem with her priorities. For instance, she wasn't home when I went to my prom. When I was a high school sophomore, I was inducted into the honor society. My mom went on a date instead of coming to see me recognized as one of the ten most outstanding sophomores in my school. Little things like that built up resentment in me before my kidnapping.

The night I was kidnapped, my mom was out on a date. When I didn't come home, she just assumed I had gotten home safe and was spending the night with my grandparents, who lived next door to us. I was angry because she didn't know until the next day that I was gone. I harbored that anger for a long time. But I finally realized I needed to accept my mom as she was.

How did you make peace with God?

I made a conscious decision to rededicate my life to God. My husband, Brad, and I were dealing with some significant issues. Whenever we were at church, our Sunday school lesson or the worship service had a message that seemed tailor-made for us. After the service, we'd sit for a long time in our car; we couldn't even drive away. The messages spoke directly to what we were dealing with. They were so powerful.

That teaching made me realize that God had *not* abandoned me. Suddenly I realized that if God was here now and cared about all the things that were going on, chances are He was there all along. That's when I finally put my life completely back in His hands.

What was the result?

Since I totally surrendered to God, I have become much more accepting and loving. I'm still strong-willed. I still say what's on my mind. But I don't attack or force my beliefs on people.

I know now that God has forgiven me for my bad choices, and He has wiped the slate clean. Even though I've been able to forgive Robert Willie and Joe Vacarro, I don't think it's possible for me to forget what they did to me. But while God knows everything that we've done, He treats us as though He has totally forgotten it. I know that no matter what someone has done, God wants that person to spend eternity with Him.

Knowing I'm important to God keeps me from focusing on my past; instead, I focus on His presence in my life. I look at the incredible husband God has given me and our two beautiful children. That's God's way of saying, "You're mine, and you're okay now."

—By Jane Johnson Struck, editor of *Today's Christian Woman*.
From *Today's Christian Woman*, May/June 1999.

Extending Forgiveness

Forgiving someone who has hurt you is incredibly difficult. Here are some ways to help you through that process.

1. *Understand that forgiveness is a redemptive response.* Only those who have purposely wronged and wounded us are candidates for forgiveness. If people injure us accidentally, we excuse them.

2. *Forgiveness requires action.* First, we surrender our right to get even. We entrust the matter to God and often choose to live with the scales unbalanced. Second, we rediscover the humanity of our wrongdoer. When we forgive, we rediscover that the person who wronged us is a complex, weak, confused, fragile person, not all that different from us. Third, we wish our wrongdoer well. We not only surrender our right for revenge; we also desire good things for the person. We bless him. This is how God forgives us.

3. *Forgiving takes time.* God can forgive in a single breath, but we need time.

4. *Forgiving doesn't mean forgetting.* The more we try to forget being hurt, the more we remember. But we can refuse to let the wrong control our lives.

5. *Forgiving can lead to reconciliation.* There can be no reunion without forgiving, but there can be forgiving without reunion. An offender who has violated a law must endure the judicial consequences. But the offended person can seek full reconciliation on the other side of justice.

—By Lewis B. Smedes. Adapted from *The Art of Forgiving: When You Need to Forgive and Don't Know How* (Ballantine, 1997). Used by permission.

"I began taking laxatives and popping pills to get rid of the extra weight."

TODAY'S CHRISTIAN

woman

March/April 2001

Need a Friend?
5 Great Ways
to Connect

You and
Your Money:
Do you have a
love/hate
relationship?

SPIRITUALLY
SINGLE?
Here's hope!

worship leader Darlene Zschech

on the Power
of *Praise*

U.S. $3.95 Canada $5.50

AOL Keyword: TodaysChristianWoman
www.TodaysChristianWoman.net

Darlene Zschech:
The Way to Survive Loss

A ustralian worship leader Darlene Zschech (pronounced "check") wrote "Shout to the Lord" in 1993 during a rough patch. Darlene and her husband, Mark, had two babies, and with a struggling motorcycle-parts business, money was tight. On a particularly stressful day Darlene snuck into the toy room where the piano was and put into song the spiritual truths to which she desperately clung: "Mountains bow down and the seas will roar at the sound of Your name," and "Nothing compares to the promise I have in You."

"Shout to the Lord," was released by Hillsong Music Australia, the praise and worship label of the 10,000-member church in Sydney where Darlene serves as worship pastor. In 1996, it became the title cut of a gold-certified worship album released in the U. S. by Hosanna! Music. Since then, the song has been sung by congregations worldwide. It has been performed for the pope at the Vatican and for the president of the United States.

What impact did becoming a Christian have on your life?

My mum and dad split up when I was thirteen. I'd already been through quite a bit, so learning about God's unconditional love took my breath away. It was the first time I fully realized I didn't need to perform or please others to earn acceptance.

But I still struggled with a lot of issues in my life. I had pretty much starved myself for five years. I would gobble up formerly forbidden foods, but soon learned I couldn't eat that amount of food and stay slim. So I began taking laxatives and popping pills to get rid of the extra weight. I really made myself sick. It was so dangerous.

How long did you battle bulimia?

About four years. After Mark and I married I started changing those negative habits. Actually, Mark was instrumental in my recovery. As my faith deepened, I worked on getting rid of this stronghold in my life. But I only let God come in so far. My eating disorder was so huge for me that I couldn't quite surrender it all to Him. But Mark wouldn't let me shut him out. When he discovered laxatives in my bag on our honeymoon, he threw them out and said, "No more."

How did you and Mark go about changing the patterns of your childhood?

When we got married, we made the conscious choice to change negative patterns for the generations to come by not even allowing divorce to be an option. Of course, that's not to say we haven't made some mistakes along the way. We had a lot to learn about truly trusting each other and believing that someone else could love you over the long haul. I've had to learn to let go of secret grudges. I've had to work through unresolved anger from my childhood.

Becoming a wife and eventually a mother gave me a different perspective. I started to understand better what my mum and my father went through. I realize now that both my parents have awesome hearts; they just lost their way for a while. They did the best they could do with the wisdom they had.

Definitely. I would have benefited from a ministry like that when I was growing up. It's only by God's grace that I didn't become a statistic. When Mark and I read *A Call to Mercy*, written by Mercy Ministries founder Nancy Alcorn, and then met her several years later, we knew this organization was a great match for us. Nearly a year after we met Nancy, God provided a house here with ten bedrooms, a couple kitchens, and even a swimming pool. It's a miracle, really, that we got the place to start a new Mercy Ministry.

We have family counseling and medical centers associated with Hillsong Church. And we have a network of churches around the nation. Girls get referred to Mercy Ministries through those.

I adore our girls. And Mark and I waited a long time to have a third child since our lives were so busy. So when I had a miscarriage, it was devastating.

How far along were you?

Twelve weeks. We'd just announced my pregnancy to the church. Everyone was so excited with us. And then they grieved right along with us when we lost the baby.

The timing was difficult. It was right before I was leaving for a worship tour. I was grieving the loss of someone I knew and loved even though I'd never seen or held my baby. As every expectant mum would know, we had hopes and dreams for this child, and those died, too.

What happened on the tour?

I *know* the power of bringing to God what Hebrews 13:15 calls a "sacrifice of praise," because there were nights when I really didn't *feel* like getting up on that stage and praising Him. But I didn't want to see the enemy win. So I said, "God, no matter what I'm feeling, I'm going to worship You now. You'll have to carry me. Because of Jeremiah 31:13, I know You'll replace my sadness with joy, turn my mourning into gladness." Sometimes I needed Him to carry me night-by-night, sometimes minute-by-minute.

How did making the decision to praise God anyway affect you?

Whenever I've worshiped in times of distress, I've seen God move in amazing ways. I think it's because praising God requires more faith even than prayer. Worship requires obedience . . . it requires an act of your will. More than anything else, God wants our heart in good times and bad. I've learned the power of that truth firsthand.

—by Camerin Courtney, managing editor of *Today's Christian Woman*. From *Today's Christian Woman*, March/April 2001.

Conquering an Eating Disorder

If you suspect someone you love has an eating disorder, here are some ways to help.

- *Talk about it.* Talk with the person about eating disorders. Let her know she can talk to you about anything without fear. One of the dangers of this disease is the secrecy that surrounds it.

- *Model good habits.* If you struggle with an eating disorder, your child will be more susceptible. A mom who's always concerned about her looks and weight communicates false values to her child about thinness and eating.

- *Explore her world.* Take time to build relationships with friends of the person with the eating disorder so they'll come to you if they have concerns about the person you're worried about.

- *Get professional help.* Take her to the doctor for a complete workup to rule out other physiological causes. Test for electrolyte imbalance, thyroid conditions, and anemia. If an eating disorder is diagnosed, see a counselor for a psychological evaluation. Make sure the counselor is a Christian who is experienced with eating disorders. Also visit a nutritionist who can help your loved one plan her diet and hold her accountable.

- *Don't blame.* Don't blame the person with an eating disorder; she already is in a lot of pain. Ask God to make your daughter alert to the good things He's teaching her through this difficult time.

—By Susan Alexander Yates. From *Today's Christian Woman*, January/February 2000.

"Divorce is like a death. It's the death of what you dreamed of when you walked down the aisle."

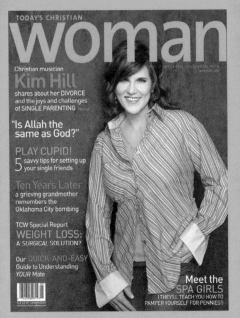

TODAY'S CHRISTIAN

woman

REAL STORIES • REAL ISSUES • REAL FAITH

MARCH/APRIL 2005

Christian musician
Kim Hill
shares about her DIVORCE
and the joys and challenges
of SINGLE PARENTING

**"Is Allah the
same as God?"**

PLAY CUPID!
5 savvy tips for setting up
your single friends

Ten Years Later
a grieving grandmother
remembers the
Oklahoma City bombing

TCW Special Report
WEIGHT LOSS:
A SURGICAL SOLUTION?

Our QUICK-AND-EASY
Guide to Understanding
YOUR Mate

**Meet the
SPA GIRLS**
(THEY'LL TEACH YOU HOW TO
PAMPER YOURSELF FOR PENNIES!)

Kim Hill: Finding Peace After Divorce

K im Hill, a Grammy-nominated and multiple Dove Award-winning singer and songwriter, began her journey in the Christian music world in 1988 with a self-titled debut that launched two number-one singles. Kim tried her hand at country music in 1994. She reached number one on the country play lists, then re-entered the Christian music scene in 1997, where she discovered a passion for worship music. She has just released a new CD, *Broken Things*, and is working on an interactive devotional for single parents and their kids titled *Hope No Matter What*.

It's as a divorced single mom to two active boys and a worship leader at women's conferences, large and small, that Kim says she's finally found the most peace and purpose for her life.

When did you first realize there were problems in your marriage?

On our honeymoon. I realized my ex-husband had presented himself as one thing while we were dating, but in reality he was very different. I'd been foolish and hadn't dated him very long. I got engaged after knowing him only two weeks. Then I got pregnant the first month we were married. So I determined to make it work.

From very early in our marriage, we went through years of counseling. We went through cycles where things got better, but eventually things got really bad again.

Did you ever doubt your faith during this process?

I thought I needed to pray hard enough and do all the right things and then God would fix my marriage. I wore everyone out trying to find the answer to our problems. When nothing worked and God didn't wave His magic wand and make everything better, that's when the bottom fell out for me. I began to question God with questions like: "Do I really trust You? Do I really believe You're sovereign? Do I really believe You care about me—because this doesn't look like caring to me." I felt hopeless and went through a serious time of depression.

What got you through those dark days?

During that season, my friend Rita Springer was leading worship at a woman's conference. I was moved when she started singing "You Are So Holy," a song she had written for a friend who had lost her baby. It basically says to God, "I don't understand Your ways, but You're still holy and sovereign."

As Rita sang that song and I sang with her, I felt my oppressive hopelessness break. My plea up to that point had been, "God, fix my marriage." During that song, I changed my focus to "I'll worship You, God, no matter what. Even if You don't fix my life, I'll still trust You, say You're sovereign, and worship You."

That was a huge turning point for me. Worship became my lifeline during this tough season. A lot of times when I was so overwhelmed that I couldn't even pray or read my Bible, I could still sing. Or I could listen to worship music and be reminded of how big God is, how there's nothing too difficult for Him, and how nothing can separate me from Him.

God promises He's near to the brokenhearted, and I felt Him near me in those moments. I knew He was going to help me. His help didn't necessarily come in the form I thought it would. But in the midst of my pain and brokenness, God met me in a real way and gave me His peace.

What was the response to your divorce?

For a while, church was the most difficult and lonely place in the world. I felt as though I had walked in with a giant "D" on my chest. Most people didn't know how to respond, so they didn't; they just disappeared. Others were judgmental; threatening that if I led worship one more time they'd leave the church. Others gossiped, wanting to know my husband's side and my side of the story.

Unfortunately, in many churches divorce is seen as the unpardonable sin. I went through a season where I felt nothing I did would ever matter again. I thought I had failed in the most important area of my life.

How did you overcome that feeling of failure?

God reminded me that nothing we do can separate us from Him. He has good plans for us. It has been so redemptive to see that what was supposed to ruin me has actually become an incredible opportunity for ministry. People are inviting me to speak and minister because I'm divorced. They know there are many hurting divorced people out there who need someone to address their needs and understand their pain.

What advice do you give to women grieving a divorce or who want to reach out to someone who is?

Divorce is like a death. It's the death of what you dreamed of when you walked down the aisle. So you have to grieve it like a death.

What's difficult is that, unlike an actual death when people rally around those left behind, most people grieve a divorce alone. So I tell divorced people to go ahead and grieve. And I tell friends and family members not to disappear just because it's awkward and they might not know what to say. Your divorcing friend needs you. Personally, I was encouraged by people who didn't try to figure out or fix the situation but who simply said, "I'm sorry." Others were a huge help when they watched my boys for an afternoon so I could get some time to myself.

What's more, there really is life after divorce. I think God does amazing, truly supernatural things through our brokenness. I'm continually amazed by the new levels of healing I continue to experience as God allows me to be part of setting other women free from the shame and guilt of divorce. The Lord continues to remind me, in big and small ways, that He is my husband and that He is in control.

—Cameron Courtney, managing editor of *Today's Christian Woman.*
From *Today's Christian Woman,* May/June 2005.

Helping Children of Divorce

In the painful aftermath of divorce, your children also suffer. No matter how good you think communication is between you and your children, there are some things kids just won't tell you, particularly after a divorce. Here are some of them.

1. *I feel so alone.* Children of divorce often feel isolated. After the divorce, they wear a smile to keep peace in the family, but inside they're miserable. Ask your child how he or she honestly feels about the divorce. Say it's okay to feel angry or sad.

2. *The divorce was my fault because Mom and Dad argued about me.* Children need to know that most arguments about them result from problems in the marriage, not the other way around.

3. *Mom and Dad each want to be my favorite parent. I feel caught in the middle.* A united front is still the best approach to parenting, divorce or no divorce. In all fairness, kids also play divorce games, pitting parents against each other to get the best deal. Also, it's easy for a divorcing parent to collapse and let the kids be caregivers. But while it's good for kids to help around the house, they shouldn't take on too much responsibility. It's not healthy for children to worry about their parents' ability to survive.

4. *When Mom tells me what a loser Dad is, I just want to die.* No matter how clear the ex-husband's faults, no matter how rotten or lousy the marriage was, a child should be encouraged to love and admire both parents.

—By Angela Elwell Hunt, *Today's Christian Woman*, May/June 1997.

"After that rape, I became very promiscuous and had another abortion. I went into a deep depression and cried for days."

TODAY'S CHRISTIAN

woman

july/august 2000

8 Great Dates
(for $10 or less)

God's Outrageous Claims
Why They'll Change *Your* Life

Running Ragged?
How to exit the fast lane—now!

Singer Tata Vega
on *making peace*
with her painful past
page 20

U.S. $3.99 Canada $5.50

AOL Keyword: TodaysChristianWoman
www.TodaysChristianWoman.net

Táta Vega: Finding Healing from an Abusive Past

C hristian recording artist Táta Vega has released nine albums, her most recent *Now I See* (Qwest Records). She has sung on movie soundtracks for *The Color Purple, The Lion King*, and *Forrest Gump*. She has worked with top mainstream artists Michael Jackson, Stevie Wonder, and Quincy Jones, as well as with gospel greats like Andraé Crouch. Yet Táta has struggled with self-esteem, anger at her parents, drug addiction, and an abusive past. Táta tells how God's transforming power has turned her life around.

Is it true that you were raped when you were fifteen?

Yes. My parents had taken me to the beach, and I disobeyed them by going alone to an isolated area behind some big rocks. As I was lying on the sand enjoying the ocean, a man approached me. I tried to fight him off, but everything happened very quickly. I was so naive, I didn't even realize what he'd done. I just knew he had hurt me.

I couldn't tell my parents what had happened. I was too scared. My father was in the Air Force, working in intelligence. He ran our family like a boot camp, and I was afraid of displeasing him. My mom told me that babies came from your armpits. That might sound really stupid, but I didn't question what my parents said.

I contracted a sexually transmitted disease from the rapist and became really sick, so my dad took me to a doctor to be treated. That's when I discovered I was already six months pregnant.

How did your parents respond to that?

My dad freaked out, then he wouldn't talk to me. He didn't believe I was raped. While my parents were with me for the birth of my daughter, they decided to keep my child and raise her as their own. I hated them for this, but in 1969, you couldn't be a minor in Florida (where we lived) and keep a baby. I didn't know that; I thought my parents should have let me keep my baby. I realize now they were just trying to do the right thing. I remember sitting on the rocking chair after Angelica was born and holding this sweet little child, feeling devastated that my parents wanted me to call her my sister. My whole life became a lie.

What finally happened with your family?

I couldn't take living all the lies so I left. I had always dreamed of going to California to become a star. So at age sixteen, I told my parents I was moving to Hollywood. To my surprise, they didn't try to stop me. In Hollywood, I ended up living on the streets. I'd sing on the street corner to make money.

One night, a man in a car offered to drive me to get some food. He seemed nice, so I got in his car. He bought me a meal. But afterward, he started driving away from the area, and I realized I was in trouble. I started to open the car door, but he said, "Don't even bother because I'll fill you so full of holes, you won't even touch the pavement." He held me at gunpoint and raped me repeatedly that night.

Did he ever get caught?

I don't know. I reported him to the police, but they treated me as though I'd been asking for it. About three months later, I found out I was pregnant. So the pastor at the church where I slept arranged an abortion for me. I guess he figured that was okay since it was a special circumstance. After that rape, I became very promiscuous and had another abortion. I went into a deep depression and cried for days. I even thought about killing myself. So I finally signed myself into a mental institution, where I stayed for ten days. Then I tried to put my life back together. That's when good things started to happen in my career.

What happened?

While I was still living on the streets, I contacted a friend who hooked me up with a singer in the musical *Hair*. She got me a part in the show. Recording artist Dobie Gray heard me and invited me to become the female vocalist for a group called Pollution—and boy, were they polluted! I went to a party after a performance, and this guy handed me a pill and said, "Take this." At first I refused, but he kept shoving it at me. So I finally took it. That was the beginning of my drug habit.

How did you escape this lifestyle?

I started to search for something spiritual to fill my void. I visited mediums and consulted Ouija boards. I talked to spirits in séances. I tried soul traveling and self-realization.

Meanwhile, I was in a band and we needed a guitar player. This guy, Jay Leach, from Wichita, Kansas, auditioned. And he was really different. We were all smoking and drinking and doing everything you could imagine, but not Jay. During the breaks when we were in the clubs, he was in the corner reading his Bible. He never said a thing to put us down; he just lived his life for God. As I watched him, I realized he had something I didn't have. And it was appealing.

Somehow, Jay got me to go to church. And on Easter Sunday, 1974, at that little church, I asked Jesus to come into my life.

How did that decision change your life?

I got off drugs, then signed with Motown Records. But there was no one to keep me accountable. So instead of trusting God to guide me, I'd meet some man and try to make him fill that void only God can fill. I'd get back into drugs and sex, and leave God behind. After about nine years with Motown, I was told I was too old and too fat, and that my career as a recording artist for the label was washed up. I was so crushed that I turned my back on God. Then I met Andraé Crouch. He had heard me sing and wanted to meet me. I went to his house, started singing, and from then on I was in his group. Andraé took me in when I had no place to go.

Is that when you met your husband?

Yes, Jeff was a musician who knew Andraé. I went after Jeff. And he introduced me to crack cocaine. The very first time I did crack, I became addicted. Then I got pregnant. Jeff didn't want to marry me, but he did, and in the sixth month I lost the baby. I became pregnant a second time and lost the baby. The third time I gave birth to Chloe, who only weighed 3 pounds, 11 ounces. After her birth, my life started to change.

One night, I walked in on my husband with another woman, and I realized I needed to go. My career had gone down the tubes, I had rebelled against God, and I didn't want my child to make the same stupid mistakes. So I left Jeff. I went back to church and started all over again. Wow, it was hard. My husband would come to visit and he'd still be getting high. So I'd get high and then I'd feel such guilt and shame.

How did you finally overcome the temptations?

God delivered me completely, but not until I confessed my wrongs to Him, Andraé, and other Christians. Then I had to say to Jeff, "You can't stay with me and Chloe any more because our lifestyles are different. We're living for Christ now."

Have you learned to forgive yourself for the past?

I know God has forgiven me, but forgiving myself has been a daily process. My past really weighs heavily on me. I have to keep believing what God's Word says in Romans 8:28: That when I follow Him, all things—even circumstances that seem like failure—work for my good. Even though God offers me mercy and grace, I still suffer the consequences of the decisions I made thirty years ago. But even in that, God still works to turn around all that sorrow and grief and hurt and shame and guilt.

That's why I love to sing for Him. For all the times I've walked away from God, for all the self-destructive things I've done, I should be dead. Yet God has kept me, and He's still watching over me today. I want to tell other women that there's a God who's merciful and filled with grace. No matter who you are, or what you've done wrong, *you* matter to God, and He can turn your life around. I'm living proof!

—by Ginger E. Kolbaba, managing editor of *Marriage Partnership*.
From *Today's Christian Woman*, August 2000.

Finding Healing After an Abortion

Wholeness is possible, say women who have recovered from post-abortion stress. Here are some key steps to healing:

1. *Don't deny your feelings.* Re-experience the abortion by talking about it in a safe environment, such as a support group, where you can diffuse the experience's volatility.

2. *Recognize abortion as sin.* Without exception, women who recovered from abortion at some point said, "I took a life. It was sin." Before you can find true healing, you have to embrace that reality.

3. *Experience forgiveness from God.* Feeling forgiven is hard, especially if you think your relationship with God is beyond repair. Lean heavily on Scripture that promises God's forgiveness, such as Romans 8:1, 1 John 1:9, and Psalm 130:3–4.

4. *Forgive yourself and others.* It's normal to be angry with yourself, your partner who encouraged you to have an abortion, your parents who made you feel abortion was your only option, or the doctor who performed the procedure. Write (but don't send) letters telling individuals how you feel—no holds barred.

5. *Grieve*. Your grieving process after aborting a child is complicated by your lack of visual memories to help you mourn. So recreate an image of your aborted child by describing the baby's physical features, emotional disposition, and personality, and by naming him or her. One woman named her child Diedre Joy, meaning sadness and joy, and wrote her a letter as part of her grieving process.

By Susan M. Smith. From *Christian Reader*, September/October 1996.

"My parents' divorce came as a complete surprise and made

me question everything. . . . I cried every day for a year."

TODAY'S CHRISTIAN

woman

September/October 2004

yoga and you:
Will it harm
you spiritually?

7 Great Ways
to Keep Off
*Temptation
Island!*

**SAFEGUARD
YOUR CHILD**
from school
violence

**Need Some
Giggle Time?**
(see our guide to
girlfriend fun!)

"Marriage Doctor" Leslie Parrott

**Working to
Make Marriages
page 36 Thrive**

U.S. $3.95 Canada $5.50

AOL Keyword: TodaysChristianWoman
www.TodaysChristianWoman.net

Leslie Parrott: Making Love Last in Marriage

eslie Parrott, a marriage and family therapist, along with her husband, Les, a professor of clinical psychology, have written several books. They've been featured on national radio and TV programs such as "Oprah," NBC Nightly News," "The View," and CNN. They've written for *Redbook, Men's Health, Family Circle, Woman's Day, Marriage Partnership,* and are advice columnists for *Today's Christian Woman.* And they've served as Marriage Ambassadors to the state of Oklahoma. Yet Leslie's own parents couldn't make their marriage work. Here are some lessons Leslie has learned about how to make love last in marriage.

What did it mean to be Marriage Ambassador to a state?

The title sounded laughably huge when Les and I first heard it. But we were blown away by then Governor Keating's heart for making Oklahoma one of the best places to get married and raise a family, even though it used to be one of the worst. We were honored and humbled that God would allow us to be part of an initiative that was so in sync with our passion for healthy marriages.

We raised awareness about the need to nurture and prepare for marriage, and we trained many professionals to work long-term with couples. We also tried to help couples take ownership not only for what was good in their relationship, but also for what was bad. We encouraged couples to avoid placing blame for problems, even if one spouse had the right to do so, because that pits husband against wife. Instead, we tried to pit a couple against the problem, encouraging them to work through the issue *together*.

Yes, we have. One of the biggest blows was my parents' divorce. It came as a complete surprise and made me question everything.

Trust became a huge issue. Les and I had been married eight years when my parents divorced. Les didn't do anything differently, but suddenly I didn't trust him or myself. I constantly questioned the choices we made and examined our interactions to be sure we weren't forming unhealthy attachments to other people. I became vigilant about dealing with even a hint of a problem in our marriage. And I cried every day for a year, when I was driving across town, when I was in the shower, whenever I was alone. I had never known grief like this before.

I spent a year in counseling, and came away with a greater appreciation for the need for accountability in marriage, and with the knowledge that no relationship can be taken for granted. A healthy marriage takes work. When we fail to do that work, we put our relationship at risk.

What's one of the best lessons you've learned from marriage?

It was freeing to learn it's normal for passion in a marriage to ebb and flow. Once I realized that, I didn't feel so anxious, guilty, and ready to place blame during those times when passion wasn't natural and easy. Sometimes Les and I feel totally connected to each other, other times we don't—that's just reality.

What issues did you and Les struggle with in your first year of marriage?

We had some major communication problems. You'd think a couple that had dated for seven years and were pursuing advanced degrees in psychology would have had a smoother beginning. But we each brought our own script into the marriage, and the other person never seemed to follow it.

Also, we're conditioned to understand, accept, and expect love in certain ways, based on the way our family of origin communicated it as we were growing up. Usually we don't even realize we have a script or set of unspoken rules until we marry and our spouse unknowingly breaks them. For example, every time Les and I went on vacation, we'd have a huge fight. We'd hop in the car and Les would drive while I opened a can of pop, put my feet up on the dash, and started singing. Les got so frustrated, and I never understood why until we spent time with his mom and dad. I discovered that in his family, his mom was the one who charted the course and handled the maps. When I failed to play that role, it drove Les nuts. But in my family, my dad was the driver and navigator; he never even wanted us to touch his maps!

Becoming aware that we even *have* these scripts, then communicating them to each other. Through counseling, Les and I learned to talk to each other about our expectations so we wouldn't unknowingly keep failing to meet them. Soon we began to create our own script for love instead of trying to live by his or mine.

We'll keep writing about marriage. There are more second marriages now than first marriages, and the issues are even more complex. There's either negative baggage from a previous divorce or the grief from the death of a first spouse plus the challenge of a blended family. People often enter a second marriage with a false sense of security. They feel older, wiser, and more experienced. But that can lead to a different set of expectations and eventually a different kind of disillusionment.

And we'll keep counseling couples. Les and I believe wholeheartedly there isn't any larger social revolution that can happen in our time than the lowering of the divorce rate. To be part of a movement attempting something so important, so huge, so God-honoring as helping marriage succeed is a tremendous blessing.

—by Camerin Courtney, managing editor of *Today's Christian Woman*.
From *Today's Christian Woman*, September/October 2001.

198

Conquering the Fear of Divorce

Adult children of divorced parents have three basic fears. Here's what they are and how to confront them.

1. *Fear of failure.* After witnessing the destruction of your parents' marriage, it's difficult to believe that breaking up is not the norm. To overcome the fear of failure, first, trust God's plan for you. Second, write down your fears, then ask God to banish those thoughts and give you victory over the sense of impending doom.

2. *Fear of betrayal.* If a parent's sexual infidelity makes you doubt yourself or your spouse, first, think about your mate's character traits and then ask which characteristics you most admire. What traits make your spouse a good risk for lifelong loyalty?

   Second, reaffirm your commitment. When you got married, you both promised to forsake all others. But it's not a bad idea to periodically recommit yourselves to maintain lifelong sexual fidelity.

   Third, meditate on God's faithfulness to you by singing or reading through the hymn "Great Is Thy Faithfulness." Trust God to help you and your spouse be faithful.

3. *Fear of abandonment.* Focus on God's constant love. Draw on the power of His constant love as you grow in commitment to each other.

—By Karen L. Maudlin, a licensed marriage and family therapist in private practice in the Chicago area. From *Marriage Partnership*, Spring 2000.

"Bringing my vulnerable baby into such a scary world terrified me.... I became paralyzed by fear."

TODAY'S CHRISTIAN
woman

REAL STORIES · REAL ISSUES · REAL FAITH

MARCH/APRIL 2006

SINGER/SONGWRITER
SARA GROVES
How she moved from
fear and doubt to
faith and action. PAGE 18

MAKE THE
BEST of Your
Empty Nest

Confessions
of an E-Bride

**ATLANTA HOSTAGE
Ashley Smith**: How God
used her abductor to help
her find freedom

**IS YOUR HUSBAND
TOO PASSIVE?**
Help him break out of the
"NICE GUY" SYNDROME

**What Kind
of Prayers
Move God?**

U.S. $3.95 · Canada $5.50

"HOW SALSA DANCING
REVOLUTIONIZED
MY MARRIAGE"

Sara Groves:
Working Through Doubt

F ive years ago, Christian singer and songwriter Sara Groves had had it. Like the prophet Jonah in the Bible, she didn't want to do anything great for God. She just wanted to be left alone.

"One day in frustration, I said to God, 'Jonah—what was that about?'" Sara said. "'You chase the man down, and you get him swallowed by a fish? He doesn't want to go to Nineveh.'" I felt just like Jonah. I was tired, filled with questions and fears. I felt swallowed up by a big tour bus. Sometimes I didn't want to go minister to people, either. "Leave Jonah alone," I told God. "And, by the way, leave me alone, too."

This was a surprising turn of events for the good girl who had become a Christian at age four, released five critically acclaimed Christian albums, one of which was named 2005 Album of the Year by *CCM Magazine*, and had made a name for herself with faith-affirming lyrics in hits such as "First Song That I Sing," "All Right Here," and "How Is It Between Us." Shortly after she had her baby, Kirby, however, Sara hit the wall of doubt.

What happened after Kirby was born that triggered your doubts?

Several of my close friends and family members had experienced tragic losses. Bringing my vulnerable baby into such a scary world

201

terrified me. I was so worn out from a rigorous touring schedule that I had no reserves left to handle this struggle. I became paralyzed by fear.

So many "what ifs." Before I had Kirby, I worried what if we were nearing the end of the world and what if bacteria were getting stronger and we were becoming more immune to antibiotics. I worried what if computer hackers stole my identity and bought weapons of mass destruction with my Visa.

After I had Kirby, my worry expanded to include what-if abductions, food allergies, and the pond in our backyard. I feared something would happen to my son. I'd always told the Lord, "Your will, not mine. Take me, make me, break me." But when Kirby was born, it seemed impossible to say, "Take him, make him, break him." I didn't trust God at that level. I told a girlfriend, "If something happens to Kirby, I don't know if my faith will survive." I realized if I could envision a scenario in which my faith wouldn't survive, then it wasn't surviving now.

Did you have doubts about God?

I never doubted God existed; I just wasn't sure about His character. It was difficult to understand His sovereignty in the face of awful things that happen in our world. I was frustrated and afraid. I didn't pick up my Bible for about a year.

What finally changed?

I got sick of myself, really. I realized the fruit of my anger was bitterness, cynicism, fear, and death.

Once, in my frustration, I argued with God about how He treated Job after his suffering. (Note: The biblical Job had lost everything: his

202

children, possessions, and health before God ended the suffering and gave him more children.) "You don't just give Job a second family and then it's all better," I said to God.

Soon after a substitute bus driver, Dick, drove us to a concert in Georgia. At one point, I chatted with him about his family. He had lost his only son in a tragic accident. Dick and his wife eventually joined a ministry called Helping Hands, which brings terminally ill children from other countries to the United States to get whatever medical treatment they need. Dick and his wife nurse these kids to health and send them home.

Eventually they adopted one of the kids, Brandon. At the end of our conversation Dick said, "If I hadn't lost my son, I never would have met Brandon—and I can't imagine life without him."

That night, I felt God say, *Sara, you go tell Dick the second family doesn't cut it.* I realized then that Dick knew something about depending on his Maker that I had yet to understand.

How did that conversation affect you?

I picked up my Bible again. I started reading Job, then flipped over to Psalms. I couldn't get enough. And I haven't stopped since. Something broke open inside me.

Soon after that I discovered I was pregnant again. I wanted to set things straight before this new child arrived. My brother-in-law Mick suggested we name the baby Toby, or Tobias, which means, "the Lord is good."

I told my husband, Troy, "The birth of our first child caused me to start questioning, so I'm going to say this questioning is finally over with the birth of our next child." I feel like I had dedicated

Kirby to the Lord, but I had never really given him over to God. At Toby's dedication, I gave both of my sons to God. In the end, this journey has been a gift to me.

How so?

The Lord helped me gain deep within my heart a greater understanding of His nature. God is good. Michael Card, in his wonderful book *A Sacred Sorrow*, says doubts are actually a profound statement of faith because they're a person saying she won't let go of a good God in the face of the profound evil she's seeing.

When I questioned God about Jonah, telling Him to leave Jonah—and me—alone, I eventually felt God tell me to ask Him about Nineveh. And I thought, *Well, Nineveh was an evil place.*

God continued, *And what happens in evil places?*

I thought, *Little girls get abducted from their own stoop. People are awful to each other. There is war and famine.*

And God said to me, *That's why I sent Jonah. I was being personal to a little girl in Nineveh, to a hurting woman there. I was running to their rescue. But I need people to do that. I need you.*

I've come to see that's the good news. Despite our depravity and selfishness, God uses us to heal people in this broken world. That's pretty amazing.

—By Camerin Courtney, managing editor of *Today's Christian Woman*. From *Today's Christian Woman*, March/April 2006.

Finding God in the Doubts

God calls us in a real world. He doesn't communicate by performing tricks. He doesn't communicate by stacking stars in the heavens or reincarnating grandparents from the grave. He's not going to speak to you through voices in a cornfield or a little fat man in a land called Oz. There is about as much power in the plastic Jesus that's on your dashboard as there is in the Styrofoam dice on your rearview mirror.

It doesn't make a lick of difference if you are an Aquarius or a Capricorn or if you were born the day Kennedy was shot. God's not a trickster. He's not a genie. He's not a magician or a good-luck charm or the man upstairs. He is, instead, the Creator of the universe Who is right here in the thick of our day-to-day world. Who speaks to you more through cooing babies and hungry bellies than He ever will through horoscopes, zodiac papers, or weeping Madonnas. . . .

God speaks in our world. We just have to learn to hear Him.

Listen for Him amid the ordinary.

Need affirmation of His care? Let the daily sunrise proclaim His loyalty.

Could you use an example of His power? Spend an evening reading how your body works.

Wondering if his Word is reliable? Make a list of the fulfilled prophecies in the Bible and promises in your life.

—By Max Lucado. From *And the Angels Were Silent*
(W Publishing, 2002). Used with permission.

"While I was modeling, I was miserable. I had no energy. Dieting even affected my personality."

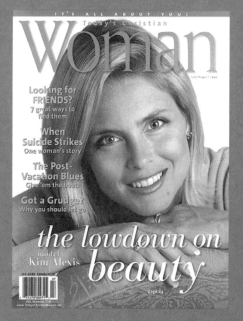

IT'S ALL ABOUT YOU!

Today's Christian

Woman

July/August 1999

Looking for FRIENDS?
7 great ways to find them

When Suicide Strikes
One woman's story

The Post-Vacation Blues
Give 'em the boot!

Got a Grudge?
Why you should let go

the lowdown on
model
Kim Alexis
beauty

U.S. $3.95 Canada $5.50

page 24

Kim Alexis: Learning the Importance of Inner Beauty

S
upermodel Kim Alexis appears to have it all: an exciting career, a close-knit family, a beautiful face, and a thin, healthy-looking 5-foot-10-inch body. Now married to former New York Rangers hockey star, Ron Duguay, they have five children, two apiece from their first marriages, and one between them. Kim reveals what she's learned about beauty, self-esteem, and spiritual fitness.

How did your modeling career affect your self-esteem?

The constant pressure to look and dress a certain way to present a certain image made me feel insecure and vulnerable. At first I didn't realize how unrealistic that image was. When I was only seventeen, John Casablancas, the head of Elite modeling agency in New York City, pursued me to become a model. After I finally agreed, he said something that totally shattered me: "By the way, Kim, you need to lose fifteen pounds." I had never given any thought to my figure before, and I certainly wasn't overweight. I was an athlete who was already lifting weights and swimming five-and-a-half hours a day for my high school swim team. That comment punched a hole in my self-esteem.

What did you do?

The only way I could drop fifteen pounds was by starving myself. I began trying every fad diet around. If I didn't drop ten pounds in a week, I was on to the next diet. My metabolism got messed up. As a result, like other models who have to diet to maintain their image, I lost my period for two years.

At what point did you finally wake up and say, "This is hurting my body, my health"?

It has been a slow process. While I was modeling, I was miserable. I had no energy. Dieting even affected my personality. Even today, I hear that little voice inside me that tells me I need to lose fifteen pounds even though I'm perfectly fine the way I am. I try to think about what I eat because I want to eat healthy, since it affects my ability to be a good wife and mother. I want to be the kind of person God wants me to be.

What's your definition of true beauty?

It's what God's definition is: true beauty is an attitude of the heart. True beauty is that sparkle in the eye of the knowledge of Christ. Obviously what the world sees is the outer surface—skin that's going to become dust some day.

What are some ways you teach your children to be spiritually fit?

I try to model a Christian life for them. It's the little daily examples of what I do that make an impact. For example, this morning my little one, Noah, woke up really early during my study time and saw me reading the Bible. So we started talking about it.

I also pray with my kids before we eat, at bedtime, and at other times during the day. If we see an ambulance, we pray for the people in the ambulance. And we try to practice thankfulness. The kids will pray, "Thank you, God, for the light bulbs. Thank you, God, for airplanes. Thank you for this air." We'll see a flower and I'll ask them, "Who made that?" Or we'll talk about what we see on TV.

Plus we've chosen to have our kids attend Christian schools and learn from the Bible there, so it reinforces what we teach them at home.

How do you stay spiritually fit?

Because I travel for work and drive my kids to and from school or sports, I spend a lot of time in my car. So I listen to Christian praise music. I read the Bible every day, and make talking to God a priority. My family and I attend church regularly. I'm also involved in Bible Study Fellowship.

I try to put God first in all situations. I'm not perfect, but I'm learning. But the more you make yourself have quiet time with God, the more you find yourself wanting to spend time with Him.

How do you feel about getting older?

I don't worry about it any more. Thirty-eight was my turning point. Earlier, before I was a Christian, having the looks and a low weight was preeminently important because it guaranteed my career and my ability to pick and choose the jobs I wanted. But today I feel my mortality more. I can't control my body in terms of trying to look like I did in my twenties. As I age and lose some of those looks, I've discovered I have to rely more on the inside Kim and the eternal Kim. Before I was a Christian that was scary. Even as a Christian it's been scary. But I've been maturing inside and out.

I want to attract people not to me but to my wonderful friend
Jesus. He's taught me to accept who I am. I'm not a young supermodel
anymore. I can see those little lines when I smile, and they're not much
fun to look at. But I want to be remembered for more than my looks.
I want people to see what's on the inside—Jesus.

—by Ginger E. Kolbaba, managing editor of *Marriage Partnership*.
From *Today's Christian Woman*, July/August 1999.

Tips for Getting Fit

Here are six things you can do to improve your health and fitness while liking yourself in the process.

1. *Avoid fitness hype.* Observe fitness industry images with detachment, reminding yourself the best reason to exercise is to stay healthy.

2. *Keep track of your efforts.* Record your exercise so you can discover what works best for you. It's motivating to see results from the efforts you make toward better health.

3. *Make deals with yourself.* When you don't have the energy to tackle a twenty-minute walk, give yourself permission to do only five minutes. Usually a five-minute walk will turn into twenty minutes.

4. *Find a coach.* A trainer can design a safe and effective exercise program for you. Look for a professional with certification from ACSM (the American College of Sports Medicine), NASM (the National Academy of Sports Medicine), ACE (American Council on Exercise), or another nationally recognized fitness trainer organization.

5. *Make exercise enjoyable.* Choose an activity you look forward to doing; otherwise it won't become a consistent part of your life.

6. *Give yourself permission to start over.* When it comes to exercise, nothing's more defeating than an all-or-nothing attitude. Remind yourself that you can negotiate your goals as often as necessary.

—By Ruth McGinnis, certified personal trainer and author of
Living the Good Life: Simple Principles for Strength, Balance, and Inner Beauty (Revell, 2001)
and *Breathing Freely: Celebrating the Imperfect Life* (Revell, 2002).
From *Today's Christian Woman*, September/October 2002.

"I knew my husband's condition was serious. Doctors don't usually call from a cell phone at night with good news."

TODAY'S CHRISTIAN

woman

January/February 2003

Are You a Resolutions Dropout?
Here's hope!

3 Great Ways to Deepen Your Prayers

Need a Friend?
9 tips to help you connect

Faith-Boosters
for Facing the Future

cookbook author Dawn Hall on

Surviving Grief with Grace

page 34

U.S. $3.95 Canada $5.50

AOL Keyword: todayschristianwoman
www.TodaysChristianWoman.net

Dawn Hall: Learning to Live with Loss

ow-fat cookbook author Dawn Hall married her high-school sweetheart, Tracy, in 1984. Tracy was diagnosed with a brain tumor in 1994. He lost his battle for life six years later, leaving Dawn to raise their teenage daughters alone. Dawn talks about how God strengthened her throughout her husband's illness and death, helping her triumph over tragedy.

When did you first realize something was wrong with your husband?

Tracy had a seizure and trouble with his balance in the fall of 1994. It took three weeks of my nagging before he went to see a doctor. I knew his condition was serious when the physician called us Friday night to tell us he wanted to see us in the hospital the next day. Doctors don't usually call from a cell phone at night with good news.

How did Tracy react to the diagnosis of brain cancer?

With shock, disbelief, and tears. I had only seen him cry once before. Then he really began focusing on his faith. Many people say cancer either pulls you away from God or draws you closer. It definitely drew Tracy closer.

Over time, Tracy's cancer improved as a result of experimental therapy. He got to where he was even bicycling thirty miles in a day. But his medical condition took a turn in 1999. It came to the point where I was shaving him, showering him, and rolling him over in bed.

In 2000, Tracy went into hospice care. He began another type of experimental treatment using blood-thinning medication and rallied enough so they kicked him out of hospice. He was doing much better; he was driving and walking around with a cane. I'd tease him, "Babe, you're going to be chasing me around the house soon!" But then he died.

What prompted your interest in nutrition?

Food addictions run in my family. I was born watching my weight. I taught aerobics at a local health club and started a group called WOW: "Watching Our Weight." The WOW group followed a twelve-step model similar to that of Overeaters Anonymous.

I stopped teaching those classes when Tracy was diagnosed with cancer, but my WOW students encouraged me to compile my low-fat recipes into a cookbook. I didn't know how to type; I didn't even know how to use a computer. I saved my handwritten recipes on top of our refrigerator.

Soon after, God prompted me to write the book for a fundraiser. We had to come up with $100,000 for the treatments that my husband's medical insurance wouldn't cover. We had $3,000 in savings, and we spent that on our first thousand cookbooks, which were spiral-bound, photocopied recipes that someone had typed up for us. I'll never forget seeing my van loaded with cookbooks and thinking, *I'm nuts! How am I going to sell one thousand books?* But we sold every one of those cookbooks the first week.

Through friends and family. After those first sales, Tracy and I discussed our options and prayed about them. Then we decided to borrow money against our home to self-publish our first cookbook, *Down Home Cookin' Without the Down Home Fat*, in 1996.

It was a huge step of faith, but we believed God was leading us. We have since sold more than 300,000 copies of that book, and we've published five others including *7 Simple Steps to a Healthier You: A Busy Woman's Guide to Living Well* (Harvest House, 2006). More than one million copies of Busy Woman's cookbooks have sold.

That our body is a gift from God, but too often we treat it like a 7-Eleven. Cancer, heart disease, and diabetes thrive on a high-fat diet. One grandmother and two of my grandfathers died either of cancer or heart disease. My father died of cancer at age 62, and my mother is battling cancer right now. My family history is one reason why I maintain a low-fat lifestyle and exercise.

The key is to do something you enjoy. I dance aerobically in the morning, then lift weights three days a week. I eat carbohydrates the size of my fist and protein the size of my palm six times a day, and as many green vegetables as I want. I watch sugars and fat. I eat healthy 80 percent of the time, and splurge on treats about 20 percent of the time.

I got that out during my ranting when Tracy was first diagnosed. After that, I can say honestly I never asked God why again. God isn't accountable to me; I'm accountable to Him.

I also sensed that somehow God would use this for His glory. I just didn't know how. That's exactly what has happened. I would never in a million years choose to go through what we went through, but I'm grateful for the good that has come from it.

I was able to share the gospel message with the two thousand people who attended Tracy's funeral. So many people have come to Christ and are appreciating life more because of Tracy's death. I share God's Word through my cookbooks, and I am often asked to speak at conferences. People who wouldn't listen to a pastor aren't threatened by a cookbook lady.

All of Tracy's medical bills have been paid off. Now 10 percent of my book proceeds go to inner-city ministries to overcome racial, economic, and religious barriers. The rest I use to support my family.

You went through "for better or worse," didn't you?

We took our marriage vows to the max! Throughout our marriage, I never wanted to dishonor my husband. If I even so much as saw an attractive man, I'd turn my head, look the other way, and never look back. At times it was hard, because I'm a passionate person. But I wanted to be totally devoted to Tracy.

I'm glad I was, because after he died, I felt free to move on. I was the best wife I could be. That was the gift of no regrets.

—By Jane Johnson Struck, editor of *Today's Christian Woman*.
From *Today's Christian Woman*, January/February 2002.

Six Ways to Care for a Sick Spouse

Whether your spouse suffers something drastic, such as a life-threatening disease, or something chronic, such as migraines or asthma attacks, here are some ways to help.

1. *Be sympathetic.* What your spouse needs most during a tough time is your support. Express your sorrow at what he is going through. Offer to pray with him.

2. *Avoid blame.* Your spouse's illness may require you to miss work, social outings, or other events. Try to avoid compounding your mate's pain by acting as if it were his fault.

3. *Be an advocate.* The world of medicine, physicians, and insurance can be confusing. Go with your spouse to important medical visits. Help keep track of medicine dosages and precautions.

4. *Be selfless.* View your spouse's pain as an opportunity for service. That may mean endless trips to the store, taking off work, performing household chores, or spending time at his bedside, ready to serve however needed.

5. *Stay connected.* You and your ailing spouse need a support system. Don't be too proud to ask for prayer, a babysitter, or a meal.

6. *Affirm your love.* An extra dose of patience, a kind word, a gentle touch, a sweet kiss, and a soft-spoken, "I'm still here for you. I love you no matter what," go a long way to help your spouse feel better.

—By Daniel Michael Darling, a freelance writer and editor.
From *Marriage Partnership*, Summer 2005.

"I totally get it when women say to me, 'How am I supposed to spend time with God? I have four kids.'"

TODAY'S CHRISTIAN

woman

REAL STORIES · REAL ISSUES · REAL FAITH

JANUARY/FEBRUARY 2006

PRISCILLA SHIRER
Why she's drawing women
BACK TO THE BIBLE PAGE 23

In Katrina's Wake
WOMEN WHO MADE
A DIFFERENCE—
and how you can, too

**FRESH HOPE
FOR A LOVELESS
MARRIAGE**

TEEN CUTTING
Could your child
be hurting herself?

**Dress for
Spiritual
Success**

**FIGHTING POVERTY—
WHAT'S THE POINT?**

**How to
DISCOVER
GOD'S
PURPOSE
for you**

GETTING PERSONAL
Bridal showers with
an unexpected twist

U.S. $3.95 Canada $5.50
www.TodaysChristianWoman.com

Finding Time for God

Ask author and speaker Priscilla Shirer about the Bible, and she'll talk nonstop for several minutes, scarcely slowing to take a breath. Priscilla has a master's degree in biblical studies from Dallas Theological Seminary. Her résumé includes stints as a radio and TV host and corporate trainer for the Zig Zigler Corporation. She has written three books for women and has developed a video teaching series titled *He Speaks to Me* (LifeWay). Pricilla is married to Jerry and is mom to two preschoolers—Jackson and Jerry Junior. Her parents are well-known Christian leaders, Tony and Lois Evans.

Here's what Priscilla had to say about finding time to be with God.

Where do you think your own hunger for Scripture comes from?

It goes all the way back to sitting under my dad's expository preaching while I was growing up. He treated the Bible with reverence, and I picked up on that at an early age. As I've spent time in the Word, that passion has grown. I've come to realize the power for Christian living is found in the Bible.

I'd love to say I make time every day, but the truth is I don't. With two small boys, I've never found it so difficult to spend time with the Lord. Normally the boys are running all over the place, and there are toys everywhere. It's mayhem around here. So I totally get it when women say to me, "How am I supposed to spend time with God? I have four kids."

Girl, I don't even know!

Sometimes when Jerry and the boys are out running an errand, I'll play some worship music and let it wash over me. Sometimes I get on my knees and praise God, asking Him to forgive my sins and to speak to me. Then I open His Word. I might have time to read only two verses, but I pray He'll use those two verses to speak to me.

I learned a great method from Anne Graham Lotz, who advises asking three questions of each verse: First, "What does the passage say?" I paraphrase the verse in one line.

Then, "What does it mean?" I pull out the spiritual principle from that verse.

Finally, "Based on that principle, what does this verse mean to me?" For example, if the spiritual principle is "You need to have patience," I ask myself if I'm exercising patience in this season of life. This is often when a biblical truth smacks me over the head, and I realize I need to share it with other women.

What other life lessons do you share with women?

When I was in seminary, I was in an on-again, off-again, intense dating relationship. I spent a lot of my time thinking about this guy rather than about my classes. I wasn't living in the present; I was focusing on what I hoped would be my future with this guy. When we broke up for good, I realized I had missed a lot of precious time with my Savior.

Through that situation, the Lord taught me to enjoy the season of life I'm in. We often miss current blessings trying to get to the next season. And often, once we get there, we look back and think, *I should have milked that season for all it was worth because now it's over.*

I constantly have to remind myself of this lesson, especially now, while my kids are young. Sometimes I look forward to a time when they'll be able to do more things for themselves and I won't have to chase after them so much. But I realize most mothers whose kids are grown say, "I miss the days when my kids were little." I hear that and think, *Are you for real?* But I hear a lot of moms say that. That tells me I need to treasure this time and, as difficult as it sometimes is, enjoy it—because it's going to be over someday. And when it's over, my kids will never be small again.

—By Lisa Ann Cockrel, associate editor of *Today's Christian Woman*.
From *Today's Christian Woman*, January/February 2006.

Finding Time for Prayer

Here are some ways you can begin building a 24/7-prayer life.

- *Get a Good Start.* I read God's Word before the demands of the day flood in, because Scripture never fails to draw me into prayer and praise. Praying from verses such as "Lord, help me to trust in you with all my heart and not lean on my own understanding" (Proverbs 3:5–6), helps me zero in God instead of the mountains I may be facing.

- *Use Tools to Stay Focused.* To keep my mind from wandering in prayer I use B-L-E-S-S, an acronym for Body, Labor, Emotional, Social, and Spiritual. For example, I prayed today for our son, Chris, a Navy doctor: "Lord, strengthen and protect Chris physically. Give him wisdom as he cares for other's medical needs. Help him trust you in his move to Hawaii. Bring him a Christian friend while he's deployed. And draw him near to You and into Your Word each day."

- *Pray on the Spot.* With all I've got going on, I don't want to forget to pray for others. So if a friend asks me to pray for a specific need, I offer to pray with her right then. If a speeding ambulance passes me, I pray for the people in it and for the doctors who'll care for the injured people at the hospital.

—By Cheri Fuller, a speaker and author of books such as
One Year of Praying Through the Bible (Tyndale). Her website, www.cherifuller.com
<http://www.cherifuller.com>, contains a monthly column, resources,
and inspiration on prayer. From *Today's Christian Woman*, March/April 2004.

Encourage the woman in your life & SAVE 37% off the newsstand rate!

With *Today's Christian Woman* magazine she'll enjoy the inspiration, insight, and much needed laughter to bring balance to her challenging days.

From cover to cover, *Today's Christian Woman* is brimming with inviting features and compelling stories that bring a biblical perspective to her busy life. Lively articles on family, career, children, health and friendships fill every issue.

And best of all, this is a RISK-FREE TRIAL OFFER. If your gift recipient likes *Today's Christian Woman*, you'll pay just $14.95 and she'll receive five more bimonthly issues. If not, she can keep the trial issue at no cost, regardless.

What an easy way to give a gift that will keep on encouraging someone you love!
No sizes to guess! No hassles of returns! Order *Today's Christian Woman* for that special woman today!

Strengthen Your Marriage

with *Marriage Partnership*

Remember the day you said, "I do?" Remember the commitment you made to love and cherish your wife? *Marriage Partnership* speaks with candor, openness, and humor to husbands and wives who want God's best for themselves and their families.

Request your RISK-FREE trial issue today. If you like it, pay just $19.95 for a one-year subscription and receive three more quarterly issues. If not, simply write "cancel" on the invoice and return it. The trial issue is yours to keep, regardless.